CAPE MAY
TO
MONTAUK

CAPE MAY
TO
MONTAUK

Text by Nelson P. Falorp

Photographs by David Plowden

A Studio Book
THE VIKING PRESS
NEW YORK

Text Copyright © 1973 by Nelson P. Falorp
Photographs Copyright © 1973 by David Plowden
All rights reserved
First published in 1973 by The Viking Press, Inc.
625 Madison Avenue, New York, N.Y. 10022
in association with Exxon Company, U.S.A.

EXXON

Published simultaneously in Canada by
The Macmillan Company of Canada Limited
SBN 670-20324-6
Library of Congress catalog card number: 72-12061
Printed in U.S.A.

ACKNOWLEDGMENT

Macmillan Publishing Co., Inc., Macmillan Company of
Canada Ltd. and Mr. M. B. Yeats: From "The Fisherman"
from *Collected Poems* by William Butler Yeats. Copyright
1919 by The Macmillan Company, renewed 1947 by Bertha
Georgie Yeats.

Contents

Author's Note

There is a marine insect (*Anurida maritima*) which can carry a bubble of air down with it below the water while it scavenges. In scavenging along this coast I have found many books to help me breathe in what at times has been a most oppressing atmosphere. Some of them are: Charlton Ogburn, Jr.'s *The Winter Beach,* which covers the whole Atlantic coast; *Whale Off* by Everett J. Edwards, which deals with the fishing off the back side of Long Island; Robert Payne's *The Island* (about Gardiners Island); John Kieran's *Natural History of New York;* Joseph Mitchell's *Bottom of the Harbor;* Elizabeth Barlow's *The Forests and Wetlands of New York City;* Robert Boyle's *Hudson River: A Natural and Unnatural History;* George H. Moss, Jr.'s *Nauvoo to the Hook: The Iconography of a Barrier Beach;* Henry Charlton Beck's *Jersey Genesis* (about the Mullica River); Witmer Stone's two-volume *Bird Studies at Cape May;* and C. Brooke Worth's *Of Mosquitoes, Moths and Mice* (about Cape May).

Other books dealing with special aspects of this coast or similar coasts are: John M. Kingsbury's *Seaweeds of Cape Cod and the Islands;* John Hay's *The Run* (about the alewife) and *The Great Beach;* John and Mildred Teal's *Life and Death of the Salt Marsh;* William Niering's *Salt Marsh Ecology;* and geologists Francis P. Shepard and Harold R. Wanless's *Our Changing Coastlines.*

Finally there is the introduction to W. H. Hudson's encyclopedic *British Birds,* which concludes with the following:

> *Let us imagine the case of a youth or boy who has read and re-read half a dozen long histories of some one species; and, primed with all this knowledge, who finally goes out to observe it for himself. It will astonish him to find how much he has not been told. He will begin to think that the writers must have been hasty or careless, that they neglected their opportunities, and missed much that they ought not to have missed; and he may even experience a feeling of resentment towards them, as if they had treated him unfairly. But after more time spent in observation he will make the interesting discovery that, so long as they are watched for, fresh things will continue to appear. The reflection will follow that there must be a limit to the things that can be recorded; that the life-history of a bird cannot be contained in any book, however voluminous it may be; and, finally, that books have a quite different object from the one he had imagined. And in the end he will be more than content that it should be so.*

7

Introduction
Hey, We Live Here

It is one of those dangerous half-truths that the enemy is us. Some of the large-scale changes proposed for the coastline between Cape May and Montauk could well alter this stretch of coast almost beyond imagination, and probably most of these proposals will never be submitted to public vote. Yet between these two points there are still many relatively unspoiled areas, and if we can talk about some of them in this book and show pictures of them without encouraging people to think that these are enough, that there are no problems, then that is all well and good.

It is not our purpose here to duplicate the work of the Departments of Environmental Protection of the states of Connecticut, New York, and New Jersey, which have detailed information available on the open spaces between Cape May and Montauk; or of the American Geographical Society, which has published a series of maps showing wildlife, wetlands, and shellfish areas, with color coding indicating national wildlife refuges and seashores, state wildlife areas, parks, local and private conservation areas, proposed acquisition areas, privately owned areas, and the location of hard clams, oysters, soft clams, bay scallops, and blue crab.

Neither have we tried to become engaged in the complexities of all the local and regional environmental battles taking place along this shore. As I traveled this coast most recently, I was struck by two things about these fights. To begin with, they had a way of becoming so complex that the amateur public was unable to sort out the truth or, if it could do so, was then unable to sustain the long legal battle of attrition against those who are getting paid to wage their side of the fight. And while there are similar issues in each community, each town deals with the problem as if it had never come up before and as if similar struggles were not taking place down the beach.

This book, then, is neither a survey, an analysis, or a polemic. Neither is it a benign paeon to nature. It is an impression of the landscape—of its more attractive existing aspects—and, maybe what is more important for the future, of some people's reactions to this landscape. Aldo Leopold in *A Sand County Almanac* has shown that man's attitude toward property can evolve, as in the case of slavery. Perhaps we can evolve an ethic toward the land, too, but he warns: "An ethic to supplement and guide the economic relation to land presupposes the existence of some mental image of land as a biotic mechanism. We can be ethical only in relation to something we can see, feel, understand, love, or otherwise have faith in."

The coast between Cape May and Montauk is probably the most difficult stretch of land in the world to have such faith in, but I live here.

Maybe you do, too.

Point-of-Land
Connecticut

10

I
"Anything Can Happen in Cape May When the Wind Changes"

The view as you come whooping off the end of the Garden State Parkway and up over the bridge at Cape May Canal is joyous. Here, after a hundred flat miles of garbage dumps and oil refineries thinning into dreary pine barrens, you have finally come to the end, so it seems, of what the modern world has to offer—to be saved at the last moment by a leap that brings you into a sky opening into several times its former size. There is the sea, which has somehow caused this change in the volume of the sky—a sea on three sides. As you dip down off the bridge, you know there is now also water behind you. Fortunately you are already down past the fishing boats packed around the old draw at the creek, and are zipping in under trees where you seem protected from all that sea and sky, enclosed by silver poplar, hedge pear trees, picket fences, wide porches, pink and white althaea bushes, red tiger lilies, elderly ladies, blue larkspur, and, most of all, by gentlemen in floppy white hats who smile benignly out from beneath their white mustaches like ghosts of turn-of-the-century naturalists—which they probably are.

"Anything can happen when the wind changes in Cape May," says the old naturalist, and even without the wind changing you are out between a pair of hotel porches of chair-

11

rocking width to a beach that might have been brushed in by Monet and phrased out by Proust, but which is in fact America's oldest salt-watering place, as old in its gazebos, mansards, and verandas as the artist's nineteenth century.

The road down the sequence of barrier beach islands from the north can be, in its way, even more depressing than the route through the dumps and barrens. There is the sea on one side and the marvelous backwaters and wetlands on the other, but what we have done along the strip of land you ride on is often a model of our inability to live in harmony with things greater than ourselves. There are, however, bits and pieces of unspoiled areas: Island Beach State Park, Barnegat National Wildlife Refuge, Little Egg and Great Egg bays, parts of the Mullica River, the Tuckahoe Hunting and Fishing Ground. Behind the barrier beach from Ocean City on down there are extensive wetlands that may yet be saved. The beach road from Atlantic City south crosses a succession of inlets—Carson, Townsends, Hereford, and finally Cape May (Cold Spring). These crossings are accomplished on the backs of narrow drawbridges that rise like dinosaurs off the flat beaches. The scary effect is increased as you mount them to discover not only much more water than you imagined to have been your companion, but water in terrible fury, even on relatively calm days, as it crosses the inlet bars. It is sometimes helpful to look inland at this point to where the water, though there, is mitigated by vast stretches of spartina, brown in autumn, and sprinkled with sea lavender and red samphire as far as you can see.

If you sail down to the Jersey coast from Montauk in summer, you probably will cut across the hypotenuse of the triangle formed by the two points, staying well out from New York City and picking up the Barnegat Light Ship. From there on you can keep the low beach in sight, ticking off those dinosaur bridges, keeping them as small as possible until you round Cape May, ease off before the southwest wind, and jibe in through the inlet at the bottom of the point. Back of the portside jetty you may hear the rifle fire of trainees learning to defend the coast against foreign powers in a place where a hundred years ago grew sassafras trees six feet in circumference. There were white oaks and black oaks a hundred feet tall and big red cedar, magnolia, wild cherry, persimmon, sweet gum, plum, grape vines a foot thick at the trunk, and holly a foot wide at the ground. All this where people will tell you nothing grows that close to the sea, where now the only *Sassafras* is a government buoy tender, and where bloom chains, sinkers, stoppers, pawls, and ratchets.

Just past the Coast Guard base looms the masonry hulk of the Admiral Hotel, long deserted until its recent brief conversion as the headquarters of a sectarian college. Before it was built at the turn of the century, there were oyster beds all through here. You can't help wondering, as you listen to the boatswain's mate drawl his command to the recruit boat crew, if somewhere beneath the stir of his ash steering sweep he cannot feel the old roll and ooze of the oyster shell. In his grandfather's time wetlands covered this whole harbor and the free water was a creek winding the three miles from the breachway up back town to the canal bridge at Cold Spring Village. All through it were nested bitterns, coots, green herons, Florida gallinules, wood ducks, and clapper rails. There are still some of these birds, but the present dredging seems to favor the ego of the water skier and the proboscis of the greenhead fly.

The jetties which now keep Cold Spring inlet open have created a back swirl in the littoral at the end of the Cape. This in turn has eaten out the Delaware Bay side as dramatically as has any seacoast erosion on the American coast. You can work your way through the old shady streets west of the hotels where blacks sell local cherries from wooden wagons and the rooming-house ladies worry their corn and lima beans and walk across the Witmer Stone Wildlife Sanctuary to where the sea is eating out the old houses. These are not marsh shacks designed to be on stilts, but full Victorian seaside homes that have been propped up on jury-rigged spiles. You can climb carefully through the snow fences, sit on the dune, look out to sea, and watch the sun set through the cellars while the inhabitants reel in their intimate garments along the laundry rig, clinging to the faith that their bureau drawers will still by dawn be drier than the starlit dew.

Of course, at that time of day there can be mosquitoes even out at the end of the Cape if the wind is offshore. Back in the streets and the winding waters they are almost always a problem. During the day in the little corner stores you can exchange mosquito yarns as you can review baseball scores, sex scandals, or mugging stories in other regions.

Tourists lie out on the beach between stone groins which were designed to retard the slipping away of America's oldest resort, but which some experts say may actually be speeding the erosion. There are wooden lifeboats on carts attended by well-trained crews of tanned young men, and signs along the boardwalk to guard against other problems of the human undertow. You used to be able to complete your feeling of security by opening one eye and seeing aloft, not the ospreys of Witmer Stone's day, but the slow rolls, quick strafes, and bright chandelles of the daily DDT pilot. At the time we all thought that the chief danger was to the gingerbread balconies and mansards of the hotels, and that if we could just somehow escape a fallout of ailerons and ridgepoles we would be safe against being lulled to eternal sleep by any implications of the evening insect hatch.

Now the spray mixture is allegedly a bit safer; at least the mosquitoes find it no worse than the previous ones. Folks say there are still nights out on the boardwalk when you can gain five pounds in one breath. The New Jersey mosquito has been at Cape May for as long as the old open verandas, and you have to wonder what the Citronella Age did about them to make life possible outdoors in those wicker rockers when we, despite all the aerial maneuvers, need to hide behind glass. According to C. Brooke Worth, who before he bought a farm in Cape May County worked on mosquitoes in such exotic places as Florida, India, South Africa, and Trinidad, part of the problem has to do with the new methods of the salt-hay farmers.

Salt-hay farming has always been important to the economy of the Atlantic coast, from Plum Island, Massachusetts, south. Relatively cheap to harvest, easy to schedule in with other coastal occupations, such as shell fishing, dry farming, and cider pressing, salt-hay farming has managed, like Shakespeare, to survive as something of value down through the years and the changing needs of the economy, and it is now used to protect green concrete. Modern salt-hay farmers do less shell fishing and dry farming and do not make their own booze, and so they need to realize a more intense investment from their wetlands. By making dikes, they are able to retain the monthly high tides in their wetlands for the entire season. The added irrigation increase helps the crop 100 per cent. Diking also eliminates the pattern of the killifish, who feed on mosquito larvae. With the bird

13

population reduced by spraying, concrete, and other related activities, the mosquitoes are free to breed in geometric progression.

In fairness to the farmer, he is under heavy pressure from a combination of developers, taxmen, and the Chamber of Commerce to convert "useless and dangerous" areas into something "profitable."

If Jamaica Bay, as we shall see, is important to bird migration, think of the significance of Cape May, sticking down as it does into Delaware Bay to the latitude of Washington, D. C. Since the days of Alexander Wilson, America's first great naturalist, Cape May has been not only the nation's first summer resort but also one of the first areas where we achieved ecological awareness, as if the southern half of the state were somehow trying to atone for the sins of the northern. Audubon worked at Cape May and north at Egg Harbor and was followed by an unbroken chain of famous naturalists up through Witmer Stone, whose two-volume work *Bird Studies at Cape May* has influenced such contemporary writers as Roger Tory Peterson, Roger Barton, and C. Brooke Worth. *Bird Studies at Cape May* is not only about birds, but about all of the flower and fauna of the region. It is not only encyclopedic but literary—witty, vivid in detail, emotionally committed, and aware of ultimate connections.

The Witmer Stone Wildlife Sanctuary at Cape May is just back of the lighthouse. Although birds are found in great numbers all over town during the migrations, it is here that they congregate now as they did in the early part of the century when the great naturalist was making observations with his cohorts of the Delaware Valley Bird Club. It was here, too, that naturalists witnessed the phenomenon of squadrons of birds flying north in the fall, in off Delaware Bay and the ocean, to land at Cape May. This puzzled them until they correlated the maneuver with the influence of the northwest wind common at that time of year. The birds, it seems, actually were flying south at night, at very high altitudes. At dawn they found themselves being pushed southward, but in a manner that perhaps made them fear they were losing control, so they would come about and haul the hard but disciplined course back upwind to Cape May. There they would settle until the wind shifted southwest; then they would take off into it and work their way south against the grain again.

Not only is Cape May the focus of the major Eastern migrations of birds, but insects, too, would come to our lighthouse a good two miles offshore. We had, of course, our household pets—flies and cockroaches—but what made our real delight was the occasional visit of a whole traveling festival of garden bugs. Usually these creatures came for only a day, and if that was *their* day, no other kind of bug would be aboard. One morning I'd blink the screen door open to find the gallery rail, the iron wall, the windowsills, fuel tank, ladders, even the knotted man ropes that swayed up to our sleeping quarters to act as fire escapes, every surface that was not sea, everything hard, occupied by a soft layer of red ladybugs. Another morning the boatswain would have the morning watch and come rushing in with his coffee cup, his hands, and his hair all dancing feelers, legs, and wings. "Lookit here, Falorp, they's all tarned yaller." Each morning in late summer it would be a treat to see what the wind would bring, and we'd duly debate and enter the Bug of the Day in the log.

14

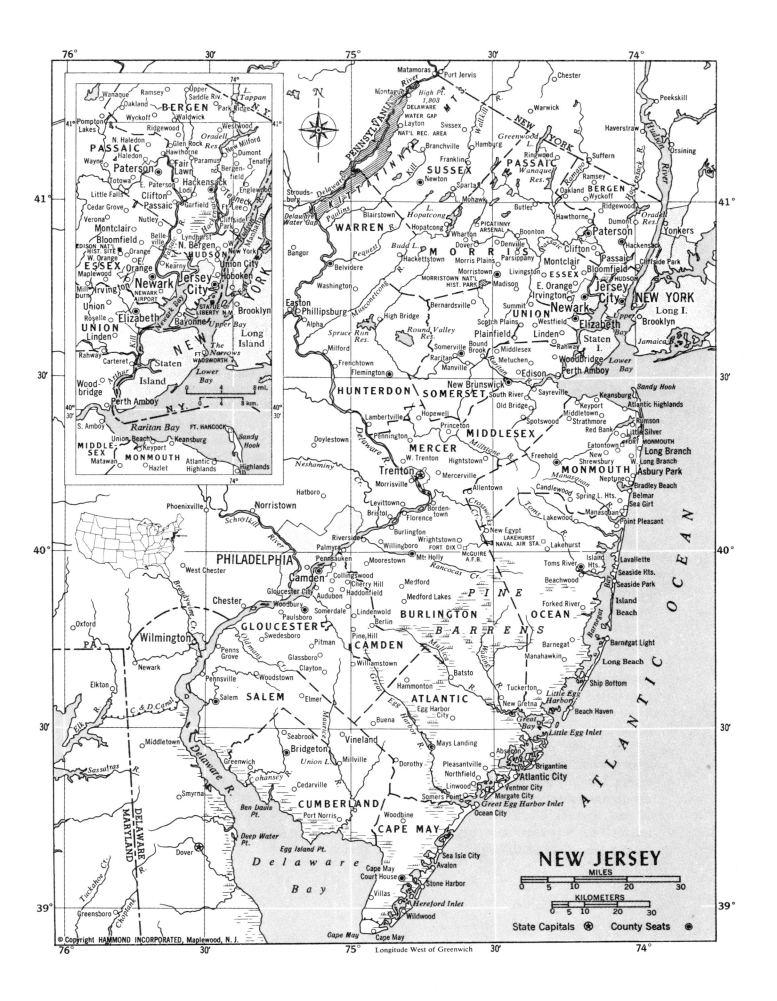

NEW JERSEY

State Capitals ⊛ County Seats ◉

Longitude West of Greenwich

© Copyright HAMMOND INCORPORATED, Maplewood, N.J.

II
A Man Who Does Not Exist: Staten Island

Suddenly I began,
In scorn of this audience,
Imagining a man,
* * * * * * * * *

A man who does not exist,
A man who is but a dream . . .
　　　　　—William Butler Yeats
　　　　　"The Fisherman"

Ever since reading Joseph Mitchell's *Bottom of the Harbor* ten years before, I had wanted to visit Staten Island to see if anything at all was left of the old oyster community at Sandy Ground. It had become for me a kind of combination Walden and Basin Street. Free blacks from Snow Hill, Maryland, had moved up to the island before the Civil War and, fishing in Raritan Bay and the Arthur Kill, had been able to make enough money to buy their own boats, forty-foot oyster sloops with names like *Pacific* and *Independence*. Just as important as the oystering, however, were the home gardens which supported each family. There were enough strawberries for export, and each person took care of his own trash, and one woman made all the soap.

In 1910 the water started to get dirty and typhoid cases were traced to people who had eaten Staten Island oysters. In 1916 the Board of Health condemned the beds. The oystermen went to work as janitors. At the end of World War II, when Joseph Mitchell went to Staten Island looking for wildflowers, there were only a few members of the deteriorating community at Sandy Ground who even remembered the days when their people had been able to make a dignified living off the local waters.

One such man was Mr. George Hunter, whose stepfather had been an oysterman and who himself had been a deacon of the church and a digger and maintainer of cesspools. Then a very old man, Mr. Hunter seemed to embody the whole modern history of the island. He and Mitchell had walked through the overgrown burial ground where most of what was left was left. I did not expect much, but I was interested to see if anything at all of a past in which this part of the coast had been in ecological balance still survived.

To get there I made use of one of the things that are making the old island disappear—the Verrazano Bridge which jumps The Narrows at Brooklyn. The view on this bright October day was exhilarating, and I clung to the wheel, luffing and easing with the flaws sweeping in from Sandy Hook and the Lower Bay while the radio banged an erotic song until I was no longer driving or even sailing—it was pure zoom.

I was just beginning to calm down when I looked up and saw a Monarch butterfly. Only that week, a hundred miles up the coast, my younger son had come to my bedroom early one sunny morning with a jar containing the Monarch he had been watching and feeding as it had grown from caterpillar to chrysalis. A day earlier it had emerged as a butterfly, a male, as our son identified by the black scent sack on the third vein of the hind wing. Christened Moxley, the butterfly had begun the pumping action of his big orange and black wings which would prepare him for his first flight, exercises so rhythmic and stately as to transcend the merely athletic into a realm truly calisthenic.

We released Moxley into the world from the bedroom dormer and watched as he bounced out upon the autumn air and turned south along the harbor's edge.

Monarchs do migrate, and as I sat beneath the guillotine-like tower of the Verrazano I could not help but wonder if the creature I was watching dance beyond my radiator was the one that had come of age in my son's hands. Fellow creature in any case, frail stitchers of the fabric of our old glacial isles. But surely not as frail as cables and concrete.

Staten Island, though traditionally pitted against the might of Manhattan Island, is, as I discovered, no small place in itself. I had all I could do for the rest of the day just to explore the eastern area. Sandy Ground, which I'd figured to be on the New Jersey side, would have to wait until the next day. I contented myself with driving up the central bluffs upon which sat Wagner College; Seaview, the sanitarium where guitarist Charley Christian died on March 2, 1942; High Rock Conservation Center with its glacial pond, and La Tourette Park. Later I walked along the wharves that lined the Narrows, pausing back of the pier where the standby and retired ferries lay.

They were like old theaters, their smokestacks, blunt bows, and elaborate railings in various stages of magnificent Plowdenian fustiness. On the quay an old man in pin-striped suit, vest, and cloth cap was bending over the cobblestones, unwrapping something. First the string had to be untied, then the butcher paper fingered, folded back, and smoothed down. From a pocket came a knife which proceeded to do its work in even, well-sawed strokes.

For a moment I thought he was going to make a meal of this quivering hunk of gristle and uncooked fat, but he selected from his coat pocket a ball of twine. Forming a noose with three fingers of his right hand, he slipped it around the middle of the slice of fat. At once I recognized a fellow blue-crabber.

20

"Have you been getting any here?" I said.

"Sure now," he said. "This is the spot."

I looked behind us where the layers of streets and sooty buildings piled up to the bluffs and cut off the afternoon sun. I looked below us at the dark ferries, wharves, and the sunlit skyline of Manhattan. It was true; there had to be water in there somewhere, and as the cliff fishermen of Aran three hundred feet above the Atlantic lay out their tarred line upon the limestone of the half-demolished fortresses of the ancient kings and do not look down to assure themselves of the sea below, so this craggy face before me spread his twine along the cobbles of Staten Island, and lifting the bait in three quick, widening circles, cast it over the wall while the line zipped and twitched out across the stones.

Our faith was rewarded with a splash. He indulged in a glance over the wall, but I looked up the bay toward the Statue of Liberty. Recalling the intimate view of those waters I'd been privy to on other occasions, I decided that for this afternoon's inspection the auditory sense would suffice.

As it was getting dark, I began to look for lodgings. In the town of Richmond, the principal settlement, there was no one on the street. By itself this fact might merely have conjured up comfortably droll remarks about sidewalks being taken in after dark. However, what the residents had put up after dark were steel screens over the entire fronts of their buildings. It is one thing to see this in the city, but in an island town the feeling of being under siege was overwhelming. The only question was, from whom were the burghers of Staten Island defending their property? I drove on through the deserted streets—it was eight o'clock—expecting to encounter at any moment the barbarians. My eyes darted from sidewalk to sidewalk to rear-view mirror and back to where my fingers fumbled door locks. Where was my fishing knife, made of Swedish steel? Why hadn't I brought a pistol? In fact I'd blown a chance just the week before to pick up *two* pistols. Why was I always so poorly equipped? Where was the enemy? What kind of war was this, anyway? And then I swung down a long dark, shuttered street, and there before me shining across the Kill Van Kull were the cheerful lights of Newark Bay. I wondered if in the black oystermen's cemetery in Sandy Hollow there were any war memorials.

New highways have slashed across Staten Island since Mitchell's day, when the island was crisscrossed by narrow black-topped roads, and I had trouble following his directions to Sandy Hollow.

I got away from the expressway which runs through the Fresh Kills wetlands by bouncing down a narrow road that runs through scrub woods whose evolution Elizabeth Barlow traces in her chapter on Staten Island in *The Forests and Wetlands of New York City*. These scrawny maples are several stages away from the great forests the glacier left when it stopped its southward advance halfway across the island which Jasper Danckaerts found in 1679, when "About one-third part of the distance from the south side to the west end is still woods, and is very little visited." In this virgin timber were "fine creeks provided with wild turkeys, geese, snipes and wood hens." Seventy years later the great systematizer Linnaeus sent Peter Kalm to survey native American botany. Kalm reported, ". . . the country here is extremely pleasing, as it is not so much intercepted by woods, but offers more cultivated fields." There were cherry trees and enough apple trees so that every farm had its own cider press. During the American Revolution the British occupied the island and chopped down all the forests for firewood. After the war the British and Loyalists fled and much of the land went back to second-growth timber. Thoreau spent nearly a year on the island and wrote, "The whole island is like a garden and affords very fine scenery." Frederick Law Olmsted, designer of Manhattan's Central Park, started out as a farmer on Staten Island but went broke in the nursery business. In the late 1870s the island became infamous for malaria, and Theodore Roosevelt's father and grandfather, who had summered on a farm at Fresh Kills, sold out in 1878.

The connection between wetland and mosquitoes becomes increasingly important as one goes south along the Atlantic coast. The Jersey mosquito need not be considered a threat as a carrier of any menace beyond its own immediate gear, so vicious is its bite, so large its numbers. In the middle of the last century, along the shores of Little Egg Harbor, the citizens were forced to surround their houses with bonfires as if they were under siege from so many wolves, but again my growing penchant for geographical fitness tells me that discussion of *Aëdes sollicitans* is perhaps best reserved for its ontological center in Cape May County.

The road that I was bouncing along was barely wide enough for my truck and was full of potholes, cracks, and areas that seemed no more than a loose confederation of crumbs. It was a road that was in what suburbanites would call "poor shape," but it had the merit of forcing me to slow down. I saw that speckled through the blacktop were bits of white, and I recalled that many of these old roads were originally built of crushed clam shells. On either side of me were white oak saplings of the kind that in the old days had been split and soaked to make baskets for these same shellfish.

Unfortunately this little road did not last for long before I found it axed by a multi-laned zoom complete with shopping centers and housing developments. On the other side I found myself entering another wooded area, this one with more variety, and I could see the turn of Fresh Kill' as it wandered in and out of the phragmites. Salt-hay boats used to manage that water, but it is now heavily silted. Just to the right of a housing development was a sign so modest I almost missed it:

William T. Davis Wildlife Refuge
New Springville

William T. Davis was one of many naturalists, like Thoreau, Olmsted, James Chapin, and Howard Cleaves, who spent important parts of their lives on Staten Island. In 1892 he published at his own expense *Days Afield on Staten Island*. The Davis Wildlife Refuge has in recent years become a rallying point for the Greenbelt Emergency Conference, which in turn is a kind of catchall for a dozen organizations, from the American Institute of Architects (New York Chapter), through the Appalachian Mountain Club, the Sierra Club, and the Woman's Club of New York. They have been fighting the parkways that the government in its infinite, elected wisdom has sought to push through Staten Island in order to make sense out of the Verrazano Bridge. The particular highway being pushed on the island at the time I was there was "Alternate Six," a name that tries to sound as if the proposition had been already reasonably modified five times into one of those *viable compromises* by which all of us reasonable, viable folk must live. In fact Alternate Six cuts the Fresh Kills greenbelt like a karate chop.

Presumably the median divider and the signs on this new highway would be painted a forest hue to conform to the idea of a greenbelt. Perhaps there could be a machine at the entrance, a kind of speedi-wash to spray all trailer trucks a temporary green. Green pills like those dropped in beer glasses on Saint Paddy's Day could be slipped into the fuel tanks so that as the green vehicles roared across the greenbelt only green smoke would issue from the exhausts, "Annihilating all that's made / To a green thought in a green shade."

The conservationists were planning a hike to demonstrate the physical realities of what this new plan would mean. Later that week officials from Manhattan were photographed by *The New York Times* bravely mounting the Fresh Kills dump in the style of Matterhorn climbers, and some were even quoted as being amazed at what the city had done to this island, for it is still news that Staten Island is the "away" for things thrown away in Manhattan.

Mr. Hunter's territory is not far from Mr. Davis's, and the road is still delightfully unimproved. You can almost count the clam shells as your tires ripple over the thin black-top. I was looking for the forty to fifty buildings Mitchell had reported fifteen years ago, and after half an hour of searching up and down Bloomingdale, Sharrotts, and Clay Pit Road, I had to settle for five or six houses. On the hills on either side, of course, were the developments that were indeed as Barlow describes them, "waves borne on a flood tide," but where was the individual *home* of Mr. Hunter with its lightning rods?

I did find a few long, narrow Southern-style frame dwellings that seemed to go back to the last century. As in Mitchell's description, they had a chimney at each end and a low porch across the front, and there was even one that rambled with wings and ells, lean-tos, and various porches. None, however, was "fully equipped with lightning rods, the tips of which were ornamented with glass balls and metal arrows."

On a rise of ground the African Methodist Episcopal Zion Church still stood. It was not Mitchell's white frame, but rather a housing-development brick. Mitchell advised asking at the church before visiting the cemetery, so I got out, but there was no one about and I had to set out for that hallowed ground without benefit of sponsor. Crabtree Avenue was still lined with Mitchell's sassafras trees on one side and the straggly privet on the other, but had suffered a thin asphalting since the day when he and Mr. Hunter had walked its dirt with a hoe to chop away the growth they knew would be covering the gravestones.

The ground was indeed sandy, the grass in patches, and stacked here and there were heaps of briers and weeds, as if the graveyard had just been cleaned, but it was a brutal cleaning, something like an army haircut. If I were Mitchell, I probably could have found in those brush heaps his chokeberry, bayberry, sumac, Hercules'-club, spicebush, sheep laurel, hawthorne, and witch hazel. As for the sassafras, honey locust, and wild black cherry trees he'd seen above the older graves, there was now nothing but the bright October air. I recalled that at the time of Mitchell's visit Mr. Hunter had told him the church had made arrangements with a contractor to bulldoze the heavy growth that had all but inundated the old oystermen's graves. I found most of the gravestones that Mitchell talked about and way in the back were the Hunters'—Mr. Hunter's two wives' and his

23

son's graves and his own grave, marked as it was when he had shown it to Mitchell with his birthdate (1869), but where I expected to see the death date there was still a blank. Without that final date it was almost as if the tomb were sprung. What if I turned around and there was Mr. Hunter?

I did some arithmetic. If I turned around and there was Mr. Hunter, he would be 103. I did the problem over again, hoping to reduce Mr. Hunter's sentence, but this time it looked like it might be coming out even higher, so I broke off, hoping I had not made things any more difficult for Mr. Hunter than they already were.

Back at the church I went up and knocked more loudly on the door. There was no going back now. I had to see Mr. Hunter.

When no one came, I turned, and there, moving across the narrow road, was just such a man as I had imagined. We exchanged greetings, and I explained I'd been looking for Mr. Hunter.

"Oh, he's been gone a long time now."

"I didn't see his death date on the gravestone," I said.

"He's up there just the same. The gravedigger made a mistake."

I recalled Mitchell's story about how Mr. Hunter wanted his second wife buried deep enough so he could be buried above her. When his wife had died, however, Mr. Hunter had been sick, and the digger, despite a promise to the contrary, had done what he had always done.

"For a while I thought maybe Mr. Hunter had lived on," I said, and I looked hard at the old man to make sure it wasn't just that he did not want to be Mr. Hunter. "He seemed to be a tough man."

"He's in the ground."

I asked about the houses, about what had happened to the dozens of homes and the frame church. All gone, the man said—a fire a few years back. I asked him if that many houses could have gone in one fire. He scratched his head and said maybe there were many fires. Fire, in any case, had done in Sandy Ground.

"Well," I said, "I came to see Mr. Hunter."

He looked at me and I could not quite interpret his look, so that to justify myself, the distance I had come, my baggage heaped up by the truck window, I said, "Mr. Hunter was a very famous man, you know."

"He's in the ground."

I did not ask him about the oysters.

The little town of Prince's Bay was the harbor for the Sandy Ground fleet, and in Mr. Hunter's day the fishermen had walked to work. I drove down Bloomingdale Road, and, though I would have liked to have made that walk, I was glad I did not have to do so because there was a multi-laned highway I had to manage before I got to the shore. Once past the highway, I found the town and through it the shore and a small tidal estuary marked Lemon Creek. There was a road running up to the mouth of the creek to where there had been a drawbridge. The tender's house was still perched on the bank. Next to the barrier were eight purple martin houses on poles a good dozen feet high. In a glass display case was a stuffed martin that had died in June 1961. A placard carried an invitation:

PURPLE MARTINS
ONLY COLONY IN N.Y. CITY
PAUSE   LOOK!

On another sign it said:

PURPLE MARTINS / PROGNE SUBIS / OUR LARGEST SWAL-
LOWS / ARRIVE IN APRIL AND / LEAVE IN AUGUST / WINTER IN
BRAZIL BUT / KNOW THEIR WAY BACK / TO LEMON CREEK
AT STATEN / ISLAND'S MARTIN STATION / ROUND TRIP: 8000
MILES / EGGS: 3 TO 5—WHITE / FOOD: INSECTS CAUGHT ON
WING / THIS COLONY ESTABLISHED BY / HOWARD H. CLEAVES /
STATEN ISLAND NATURALIST.

The study went back to 1953, when six pairs had nested. Later I found that Mr. Cleaves had just put up the houses that year on the hunch that martins, allegedly good mosquito chasers, would be interested in Raritan Bay if properly encouraged. His second year, fourteen pairs had nested. The high was in 1963 when there were seventy-five. Five years later the number dropped to twenty-seven. In the last two years on the chart the number had come back somewhat to fifty-six. Then I noticed that this year had not been recorded. And here it was fall. On the board there were blank spaces for the years to 1974, and there above the board were the houses. I wondered if Mr. Cleaves had stood like Yeats at Coole Park counting the swans for eighteen seasons and then on the nineteenth awoke to find that they were gone.

On the shore across the missing bridge, highway workers were eating their lunch. Up the creek, cut off by meanders, two other men perched above the phragmites on a barge with two different styles of boat cabins set upon it. A factory whistle shattered the mood, and I looked up to see not a factory but a tanker big as a factory moving just off the beach. She was riding high, but her prop was still covered so that it made no sound, and with her bow cocked out toward Sandy Hook, the effect was as if she'd been up even closer to the beach, had perhaps dropped out of the sky.

Between the reeds and the ship a kingfisher was working, his short, blurred wingbeats making a whir in the silence that was caving in all around the fading whistle. He'd go from the limb of the tree by the defunct bridge into the water and back as if he were on a yo-yo string. I had to watch him twice to see that he needed the leverage of that branch to subdue what his fine double-eye had shown him, first in flight, then without refraction, beneath the surface of the tide.

25

III
Under the Gun: Broad Channel

Why did the poor poet of Tennessee, upon suddenly receiving two handfuls of silver, deliberate whether to buy him a coat, which he sadly needed, or invest his money in a pedestrian trip to Rockaway Beach?

— *Herman Melville*
Moby Dick

One late summer day in Manhattan I found myself with some time and decided to explore the harbor. I had heard that there were still some relatively unspoiled natural areas among the complex series of bays, rivers, and islands that, after all, still make up the basic structure of that "very pleasant situation among steep hills, through which a very large river, deep at its mouth, forced its way to the sea," that Giovanni de Verrazano had discovered from the decks of the *Dauphine* in mid-April 1524.

There was a subway at Central Park, and I went down into it and boarded a train bound south for the Battery, where I planned to take the Staten Island ferry.

There is now your insular city of the Manhattoes, belted round by wharves as Indian isles by coral reefs—commerce surrounds it with her surf. Right and left, the streets take you waterward. Its extreme down-town is the Battery, where that noble mole is washed by waves, and cooled by breezes, which a few hours previous were out of sight of land. Look at the crowds of water-gazers there.

27

While I was thus meditating on Melville's hundred-year-old vision of Battery Park, my eye kept going over the subway guard, or rather his equipment, for his face was so young and frightened I could find no spot there to let my eye come ashore. After a few blocks he moved on and I saw, behind the place where he had stood, a map of the city. The land was white and there were intriguing patterns of blue all around it. There lay my goal, Staten Island, off the southwest corner of the harbor, but out on the eastern side were places called Rockaway, Coney Island, and Far Rockaway. There was Jamaica Bay and in the middle of it a number of islands. One of them carried the train right down its middle and was called Broad Channel. I had heard that Jamaica Bay was "hopeless," and I recalled some miserable experiences at Kennedy Airport when my chief fear was that we would duplicate recent headlines by crashing just short of the runway into Jamaica Bay, a place which, by process of journalistic association, had become for me the prime *cause* of airline disasters. It was rather pleasant then to indulge in an abstract study of the layout of this notorious area while at the same time bouncing along safely underground on my way to Melville's Whitehall.

The subway began to fill up. A Hawaiian sat opposite me in, oddly enough, a Hawaiian sports shirt that made him look more American than he otherwise might have. Across his lap was a transparent bag and in it seemed to be the various segments of a collapsible fishing pole. On the seat next to him was a bowling bag through the unzipped top of which protruded bright bits of fishing gear. As we neared Wall Street the fisherman was lost among a number of boarding stockbrokers. I asked one directions to insure my getting off at Whitehall, for I knew that I could end up spending the day rattling among the dark places of the earth. By now I wanted to, like Melville's Redburn, be with the crew "at last cast loose, and swinging out into the stream . . . in Whitehall boats, their chests in the bow, and themselves lying back in the stern like lords."

The stockbroker was in the midst of an accurate tip on how to escape when the door whooshed open and he was gone, cast loose with his fellow crew before I could confirm his advice. Nearly empty, the subway rattled on. Across from me was the Hawaiian. I knew that now I was, for better or worse, in his hands.

Past South Street we rode, beneath where Hart Crane had met his green-eyed sailor man with the shark-tooth necklace, and where Charlie Muller, an old sailor, had written about South Street at the turn of the century: "This was a wonderful street, with all those sailing ships at the piers, sticking their jibbooms right over the street very near to the houses opposite. And those wonderful smells! And the street hawkers selling fresh oysters and clam-chowder. . . ." Now the reconstructed Hudson River sloop *Clearwater* sails from South Street to campaign for the quality of river her kind had known when they brought in the clams and oysters or were Whitman's "hayboat in the twilight." John M. Burns, currently director of the Hudson River sloop *Restoration,* speaking for his group and other organizations like the Hudson River Fishermen's Association, has said, "I think we can save this river. And if we can do that, then we can point the way for the rest of the country and show other people how they can save their own rivers, too."

Above was the Fulton Fish Market, the end of the rainbow to which, up until the 1930s, the fishermen in my town a hundred miles down the coast would send their catch, often shipping fifty barrels of lobsters a day out of a village of eight hundred people. Now

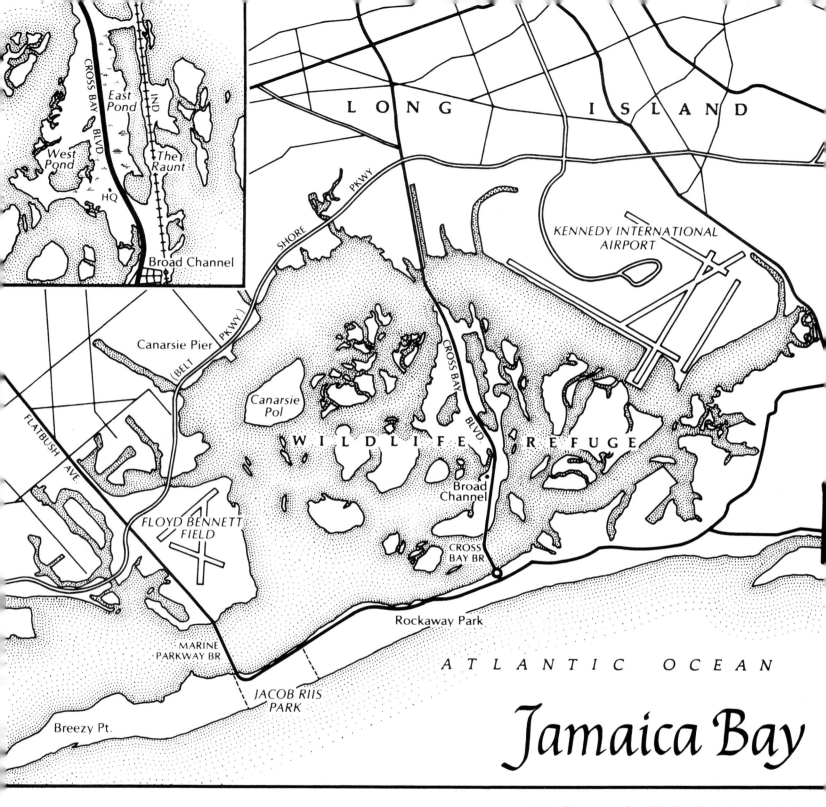

Inset map (upper left):

CROSS BAY BLVD.

East Pond

West Pond

IND

The Raunt

HQ

Broad Channel

Main map:

LONG ISLAND

SHORE PKWY.

KENNEDY INTERNATIONAL AIRPORT

Canarsie Pier

(BELT PKWY.)

Canarsie Pol

CROSS BAY BLVD.

WILDLIFE REFUGE

FLATBUSH AVE.

Broad Channel

FLOYD BENNETT FIELD

CROSS BAY BR.

Rockaway Park

MARINE PARKWAY BR.

JACOB RIIS PARK

ATLANTIC OCEAN

Breezy Pt.

Jamaica Bay

Map of Jamaica Bay by Richard Sanderson from *The Forests and Wetlands of New York City* by Elizabeth Barlow, © 1969, 1971 by Elizabeth Barlow, reprinted by permission of Little, Brown and Company.

the train no longer stops at the little fishing towns along the Connecticut coast. What lobsters are caught go to local restaurants that supplement our catch with truckloads from Nova Scotia or from out-of-state draggers working the continental shelf with nets.

Some fish, of course, are still shipped to New York. The fisherman's price depends upon how the market is the day the fish is sold. When swordfish were still being caught in numbers three or four years ago, it was a frequent sight to see them with their heads and tails cut off, stacked up like cord wood in the fly-thick gutters around Fulton Street while somebody played with the price. Fishermen can organize, and slowly they are doing it, but the temperament of a man who goes to sea in a small boat is often against joining groups.

As we crossed under the old ferry to Brooklyn, I was reading not Whitman, who had assured us "a hundred years hence . . . others" would see the same sights, nor Hart Crane, Marianne Moore, or Jasper Danckaerts, people who made this crossing variously by epic, free verse, and rowboat, but the graffiti on the flashing walls and, odder yet, the legal messages which urged my glum-faced and sallow fellow passengers on to the good life—it always seemed to be in places not on our line. My Hawaiian fisherman, however, held fast to his rod, and I held fast, at least visually, to him. I dared not look at the map, but I knew the region we were riding into was the zone of disaster.

The darkness, the noise of the wheels more horrible than that of any gull, the shrieking graffiti flying past, the sad faces about me—and then with a scream we were up into light, suddenly borne aloft not into industrial junk yards but amid spartina grass and shacks on spiles, green spartina and water, and the passengers lifted their faces and poked one another with their elbows. One, an old man with a gym bag, winked at me.

The old man next to me stood up and turned around so he could see the view out of the window as we rose on a bridge to cross blue water. I didn't dare look at the map for fear that all this out the window—and maybe more important, all that was going on inside the car—would stop.

The car did stop, but not what was going on inside, where everybody was quietly massaging the windows and winking and poking their neighbors just as if we were on the train coming up from Limerick to Dublin and some cow had crossed out of the green to arrest us.

A long-necked white bird flew past the window and glided over to a spartina island where there were two others of its kind. It alighted long-legged among them, and the old man touched my shoulder and said, "Swans," and I said, "No, I don't think so. Egrets." And he turned to his friend and said, "Swans." And I said, "But ladies' hats, extinction— it's even better they should be egrets."

"Hey," he said, and put his hand on my knee, "a good place for any bird you like."

The train chattered down the rails, off the bridge, and on through a stretch of spartina and back bays, and then there were more houses on stilts, with catwalks connecting them, instead of streets. On the roofs were galvanized tubs full of flowers. I couldn't believe in this village of catwalks. Although I'd seen boardwalks used on the sands of Fire Island, this was a real community. I was fantasizing a life of living there for at least forever, even though I knew, like everything seen from the subway, it would all be wiped away in a moment, sure as posters advertising tropical islands. Certainly there seemed to be no way for me to get out of my world behind the mass transit glass into the gloriousness of that world passing before me.

And then the train stopped.

A dog trotted along the wooden walk near my window. The planks responded to his stride. A boy on a velocipede pedaled after the dog. The only other traffic about him was the molecule-by-molecule diffusion of oxygen into the stomata of the spartina, a movement down the leaves, through the stems and rhizomes, and into the roots. Up ahead, on some concrete, people were getting onto the train. No one, however, was getting off. So it was just as I thought—not a real place at all, not a place you could *get off at* and *go to, be at,* but a place people left or flew past. I sat back . . . there was something wrong.

The seat opposite me was ominously vacant. The old swan lover was still with us, his friend, too, and the girl with the pretty legs. Who was missing?—the Hawaiian! The fisherman. Inscrutable son of a gun had fled. . . . .

Maybe this vanishing act of his was for the best—perhaps he had existed only to show me this brief moment, this vision of possibilities, and now I was to be on my own. Was I up to that catwalk maze without a guide? It was one thing to romanticize about it, another to go out into it, walk it. But there he was. Not quite yet vanished. Walking along with his fishing rod and gear bag and not a bit ethereal or inscrutable, but rather like a stockbroker with attaché case and rolled umbrella.

I rushed to the train door and just made it. In the concrete station the guard said, "Are you sure you want to get off?" He had a point; every other person was going the other way, with bathing suits wrapped in towels and summer sizzler beach chairs, bags and bags of not quite foldable, not totally collapsed collapsibles that looked all too ready to spring into the promised life on the permissible six-by-six feet of beach. And though the train was shutting its doors, they still wanted it, pressed toward it through turnstiles that grabbed at their hips, gear, and elbows like linebackers. "Are you sure you want to get off here?"

"Why?" I said. "Where is this?"

"Broad Channel," said the guard. He was, however, blocking my way.

"Can't you just . . . walk around in it?" I said. "Broad Channel—?"

"Broad Channel," he said. "Rockaway Beach is that way." He pointed across the water to where a line of chocolate high-rise apartments filled the blue. Close to us I could see the little houses on stilts; they were all around the concrete block that was imprisoning me.

"I just want to . . . get down there," I said, "into Broad Channel."

He sighed. "Well, it's too late now anyway," he said. "The train's left. You know I can't hold up a train forever."

I thanked him and passed through. Down on the street (for there was a street as well as catwalks) the Hawaiian was just passing into an alley between two shacks. I had to trot to catch up. He was plodding down a road littered with old cans and clam shells. There was water at the end of the road and signs advertising boats and bait. He went up a wooden ramp onto a catwalk that led to a large wooden staging upon which sat wooden fences and a half-dozen wooden shacks all hung together to form a kind of medieval inn yard.

31

The Hawaiian passed into what seemed to be the principal building. Outside, a large man with a beard, sailor cap, and plaid shirt was wrestling with an outboard clamped to a steel drum. Two or three old men lounged along the rail that overhung the water. Below them on the float two young men bailed out an old wooden boat. Fifty yards out on the water, halfway between us and where the concrete train bridge cut across a grassy island, a half-dozen similar boats kept afloat the hopes of their occupants.

"Porgies," explained one of the old men. "No weakies yet."

"Oh, yes," said the other old man. "Lots of porgies."

I watched the man with the plaid shirt fiddle with the outboard. He did not really seem to mind that it did not roar into life. The sun was warm, the breeze gentle. He strolled about the steel drum and nodded his head.

"Do you rent boats with just the oars?" I ventured.

"Why, yes," he said. He looked at the engine for a moment. "Yes, oars are a part of our policy."

He sent me into the shack where the Hawaiian was negotiating some bait and a sandwich. The Hawaiian did not appear to be aware I had followed him all the way from mid-Manhattan, but, to set his mind at ease, I explained to him that I had and why, none of which interested him as much as the bait he was going to use to catch porgies. The woman behind the counter wanted to know if I wanted any bait. I told her I just wanted to row around, and I ordered a roast beef sandwich.

The young men had the old wooden boat all cleaned up and waiting at the float. I thought of how it must have been back in my village when the present gas dock was a rowboat livery with fifty orange-and-white wooden boats. Each boat had a bailer and a stone anchor and the oars—two pairs if you thought your companion could keep your rhythm. The customers would row a few hundred yards out over the eel-grass flats and anchor inside the islands, or draw up on the island beaches and spend the day. At sunset the man who owned the livery would make a large circle out through the flats in his converted catboat and tow home all those whose oarsmanship had been weakened by sun, beer, or love. Now there is a constant heaving slick at that pier, especially on summer weekends as the former rowboat customers, now in possession of floating kitchens and sun porches, blast past, bound for a mile out beyond eel-grass flats that are now abandoned except as a parking lot for plastic yachts.

I rowed away from the porgy fleet along the catwalks connecting the houses. From the chart on the wall in the bait shack I knew Broad Channel Island was surrounded by dozens of smaller islands and channels with names like Little Egg Marsh, Pumpkin Patch Channel, Canarsie Pol, Ruffle Bar, Grassy Bay, and Yellow Hassock. To the east, up through the porgy fleet and the subway bridge, lay John F. Kennedy International Airport. A steady flow of silver jets about the size of my index finger kept pointing down at it, their black trails stretching out, then spilling off over the chocolate high-rises of Rockaway. Ahead, out west, was a high-arching road bridge. Beyond it were the silver skyscrapers of Manhattan. Somewhere in between was the place I'd selected for my destination, a channel running up between Ruffle Bar and Yellow Hassock on the one side, Little Egg Marsh and Broad Channel on the other—a piece of water known on old charts as The Raunt.

The wind was against me that way, and I figured I could always come back on it. I wanted to make sure I'd thought out things like that, for I had the fear of entering foreign waters, and surely these waters, though only a hundred miles from home, were more exotic than any I'd found in the River Shannon. At least one knew what products had gone into that stream, but who knew what devils lurked in these waters?

The tide was also against me, and I was not sure of its strength, especially out beyond the friendly catwalks. Somehow I had in mind a notion that the strength of the current was a function of the strength of the pollution; probably I'd picked it up on the Mississippi at New Orleans. Distances also seemed unpredictable. My timing was hyped up by the city and the subway. Out here the islands with all the wonderful names were flat, and my only perspective came from bridges, the chocolate-cake skyline of Rockaway, and the fantastic skyline of Manhattan. The fact that jets were continually popping in at Kennedy did not help my navigation.

To keep out of the wind and tide, I rowed closer to the catwalks than my normal sense of propriety would have allowed. In some cases the spiles seemed to grow out of the spartina, in others out of the ooze or the water. The houses were all fairly small; many seemed abandoned. I found myself gliding under a walk. Kids with crab lines hung off a porch. Unlike urchins in my village, they did not shriek that I should purchase an outboard, but rather sang a stanza of "Row, Row, Row Your Boat."

"I hope I don't disturb your crabbing," I said. "I'm trying to sneak through the wind."

"Row, row, row," they sang, and the blueshell strutted out of the net up there, cakewalked across the planks, and thence on overboard off my bow.

"There he goes," I said, and watched him slide into the gloom.

"Gently down the stream," they sang. . . .

A dog peered down at me. A curtain blew out above my head. At my elbow a cast-iron pipe hung from the underside of a house. Its mouth dropped something onto the mud. At home I swam daily in a river with outfalls like this, so that here, where the poisonings held such vast and anonymous possibilities, I welcomed so personal and familiar a sight.

I gave a stroke or two out of sheer joy, and the roiled water smelled no worse than the ordinary low tide which often enough is not "pollution" but the natural decay of such matter as ulva or sea lettuce. I turned to see if I was about to ram a spile, and there, like a seagull pecking about in the mud, was a snowy egret.

He was wandering in and out of the basements, as it were, and I drifted to within two boat lengths, watching his eye flash, his neck shoot, his throat quiver. He flew off, gawky in his escape down lagoon before rising above the roofs, where he turned and eased into the tall spartina behind the houses.

Under another line of houses two more egrets were stalking. My bird, then, had been no mad, jet-zonked stray, but part of a colony. Here in the midst of this human community was yet another community that formed a food chain strong enough to support the birds of a species that once were slaughtered to cater to a perverse fashion. Now, under stilts and catwalks, among spartina and blueshells instead of a world of salons and bustles, they could display their true elegance.

Working from under the houses and walks, I pulled along the edge of the channel. Out beyond me a few modest boats were moored, mostly old inboards of the kind I'd known as a boy on the Connecticut River—slow, stable craft whose builders had recognized that in pleasure boating to be aboard is to be *there*. Out farther a tow boat was bringing two more fuel barges in from Rockaway Inlet along the Beach Channel up toward Kennedy.

While I was watching the barges, a voice leaked in over my shoulder. It came from a railing along the last of the Broad Channel houses. The speaker was arranging his crutches, leaning them on the rail while he prepared to lower himself into his wood-and-canvas chair. "A good day for a row," he said.

"A good day to sit in the sun," I said.

"Yes, a good day to sit in the sun."

Ahead arched the highway bridge that took Cross Bay Boulevard, parallel to the subway, from Broad Channel over to Rockaway. Along the rail, like so many bowmen defending the battlements, were old men and kids, their poles rising and falling against the blue sky. I picked a spot between the lines and pulled in under.

It was nearly noon. After the hard row it was pleasantly cool beneath the tall canopy formed by the bridge. The current was even stronger, rippling along the bridge supports. Up ahead the water opened out to distant green shores. In the far mist were the two new skyscrapers of lower Manhattan, gleaming like cracker cans. I put the boat alongside the concrete island that joined the bridge supports, and I jumped ashore, taking the anchor line. For a moment I had a premonition that the other end had not been fastened to the boat, and I imagined the hull lurching away, bobbing out from under the bridge, swirling off while I stood marooned forever beneath the six-lane highway.

The crew at the boat livery, however, had done their job if I had not done mine, and the boat remained one of my possibilities while I unwrapped my sandwich, sat back against the bridge support, and watched the train pass over the far causeway. Above, someone was crabbing. His star-trap descended, slowly rotating, its monofilament line invisible against the high sky. I took a bite of my sandwich and forgot the crabber to watch the tow boat and a water skier who was actually braving the medium into which five metropolitan sewage plants and the world's greatest airport emptied their errors. Then up from the water came the crab trap, dancing with legs and claws, up, up, slowly into the jet path, until what I had before me was a bird cage pursuing in slow time its escaping tenant.

I had finished half my sandwich when I was startled by what I at first thought was gunfire. O.K., I thought, this is it, the end of the pastoral interlude—back to the city. Only a month before in my own village some of us had been fired upon three times while fishing from the trestle. O.K., I knew what to do. I rolled over and kept flat. Wasn't that what life was becoming more and more—no longer the days afield, afoot, but the maintenance of a low profile?

For some time I lay there, trying to taste more of the bait lady's roast beef than the highway department's concrete. There was another burst hitting the water, kicking it up in a wide pattern, the echo of the splash almost louder than the cars overhead, louder almost than even the passing jets. Then one missile jumped so high that I saw what it was—a fish the size of my outstretched hand, silver—raucous squadrons of them now. Above me fell the cries of the street boys and the old men as their miraculous hoistings of silver porgies progessed up and up until the airplanes were no more.

34

About the only sizable trees in town were along the esplanade of the one wide street. I realized with a shock that this road was actually not a Broad Channel lane but Cross Bay Boulevard, momentarily subdued by traffic lights, awnings, and trees to make a kind of 1930 Midwestern Main Street. There was Sullivan's drugstore with its tin ceiling and a post office window complete with brass boxes; there was the Chamber of Commerce, the grocery store with apples in the window, the wood-smelling general store with a brass scale for nails and a stock of Lighthouse for the Blind cleaning supplies, the ominously abandoned storefront with a ten-foot cockeyed cardboard banner saying: "Help Save Broad Channel." Next to it was an even more ominous bar front crashed in and scorched, its ruptured green upholstery and warping tan paneled walls still stinking from the char and the hose.

I went into a bar that was a little less violently decorated. There were a couple of men at one end discussing the Mets. The color TV was on, showing a peruked dude shaking his cuffs and snuff, saying, "Elba may only be a small island, but you will come to realize, *mon amie,* the King does not forget!"

In the context that was a bit too much. Even the Mets fans gave the TV a narrow eye. I ordered a draft and asked directions to the wildlife refuge.

On the way out past the Legion House with its scroll of World War II vets, I could see where a good deal of Broad Channel's trash came from. People in cars, speeding from the city to the beach like Germans and Russians blitzing back and forth across Poland, tended to see this community as, at best, an impediment to their progress. Most, as they fired their packaging out the windows, simply did not seem to realize that real people were living here, although in an easily visible lot girls were playing softball and in the space between two houses a half-dozen boys were diving off the roadside into what at first looked like an elderly lady's garden.

And there the old lady was, taking this rather calmly, merely leaning over a little farther and clipping. I walked across to see exactly what was going on and was greeted by a splash as the latest diver hit the water that so often in Broad Channel amazingly appears around the corner or under a house. The particular stretch that I could see was about the size of a good suburban lawn. It sparkled away toward a stand of phragmites and a small sign proclaiming that this was the Jamaica Bay Wildlife Refuge. I had mixed feelings about people swimming in what I assumed to be an arm of the bay, but the woman looked up from her gardening to explain that this was one of the fresh ponds created by the subway embankment project.

The subway bridge upon which I had come over to Broad Channel was, she explained, responsible for the wildlife refuge at the northern tip of the island. At that spot a branch of the Long Island Rail Road had once precariously jumped the bay on a wooden trestle built in 1877. Through the years one of the sideshows passengers traveling across to Rockaway would experience would be the bursting into flame of the venerable wooden span. In 1950 the beams were deeply eaten into by the flames and the railroad was happy to abandon its service to the outer beach. The New York City Transit Authority decided to take up the challenge of crossing Jamaica Bay, but they concluded the best way to insure their trains getting over the water was to fill in as much of it as possible beforehand. To obtain this fill, the Transit Authority requested a permit to dredge the bay bottom.

By then, however, the bay, bottom and all, was under the care of Robert Moses' Parks Department, and he made an interesting deal. In exchange for enough bay bottom to make an embankment across most of the bay, the Transit Authority would put enough bay bottom (which turned out to be fine white sand once part of the outer beach) up onto Broad Channel Island to make two freshwater ponds, one on each side of Cross Bay Boulevard, the ponds would attract waterfowl.

On the other side of the street, however, was Jamaica Bay itself, and there, poised above its edge, was a diving board. It was no jury-rig either, but was bolted to the wooden abutment of the short bridge that carried Cross Bay Boulevard over the creek. No one was swimming there, but people were fishing. One lad was attempting to detach an eel he'd just hooked from a roll of what looked like Scott's best double-ply, soft-weave. There was also a lot of grim footing along the shore as I tiptoed over the brown beach to him.

"What's that you got?" I said.

"Eel," he said.

"What's that he's gotten wrapped up in?"

The boy looked at me and then back at the smothered eel, and his face got red. "I know," he said quietly.

The houses along that stretch were all on stilts well out from the parkway. The cars were parked up by the road, and the backyard sloped down from the cars into mud that sometimes reached as far as the houses and sometimes shelved off into the bay before reaching the stilts. In order to have gardens the people followed the techniques of barge wives and used galvanized washtubs, buckets, assorted pans. On the flat roof of one house was an enameled bathtub full of red geraniums.

The refuge was up on a sandy rise. There was a low headquarters building presided over by a woman who seemed to be more rest-room attendant than guide, though she did give me a "permit." The "permit" was a pamphlet listing some of the things one might see in the refuge. It said that the birds which come to this western end of Long Island are not only the local mallards and black ducks, but more than three hundred other species, including such rare birds as the southern pelican and the redwing thrush, a European bird never before known to have come to this continent. As for the attendant, she was reading a paperback mystery story about a strangler rising from the *rank miasma*.

Pride of the refuge is the snowy egret, our friend from beneath the catwalks and along the trestle. The bird had been officially extinct in 1923. Another bird, ninety years missing from the New York area—the glossy ibis—settled its reddish-brown feathers into wading activities at the refuge in 1961. Jamaica Bay picks up many birds of many different kinds because it is at the crossroads of two important migration patterns: the East Coast flyway from Newfoundland, and the Midwestern path in from Canada and Michigan. The combination of quiet salt and fresh water and the attendant plant life encourages the birds to stay over longer than they otherwise might.

In addition to the crabs, snails, crayfish, mummichogs (killifish), and insects, the birds feed on plants, many of them imported and planted by refuge director Herbert Johnson. Through the years he has set out bayberry, chokeberry, and autumn olive, plus wheat, rye, and oats, and even a hardy Japanese black pine grown from seeds taken at Jacob Riis Park across the bay, on the Rockaway barrier beach.

I walked about the paths of the refuge and watched the flocks of birds rise and fall over the subtly colored marsh grass. Around one bayberry bush an old man with a walking stick and loud coat popped up and said he'd just seen two teen-age girls and that they were, believe it or not, *hunting bear*. We both cackled and leisurely went off in opposite directions. It was good to know that this end of Long Island, which for many years presented to the birds only the fascination of the fatal beam at Fire Island Light, could once again be of positive use to the vital migratory streamings that have been essential to American bird life since the glacier first withdrew leaving the bones of this island. It was also comforting to know that it was a place where an old bird of another sort could still make his jokes.

When I walked back to catch the subway, I paused at Sullivan's drugstore to have an ice cream soda under the tin ceiling and to write post cards to my friends saying that America was alive and well in Broad Channel. The womam who made my soda stepped behind the little barred window of the postal section. "It will say Rockaway on it," she said, stamping my card.

"Don't you have a stamp that says Broad Channel?" I asked.

She looked around for a minute and came up with one. "It will cover up your writing," she said.

"Fine," I said. "That will be an honor."

Later, in reading the reports of the National Academy of Sciences, the recommendation of the National Gateway Park Commission, and Elizabeth Barlow's chapter on the refuge in her fine book *The Forests and Wetlands of New York City,* I began to have second thoughts about the three communities—the airport, the refuge, and the people of Broad Channel. While it is true the planes threaten the birds, the birds are also seen by some as a threat to the planes, and as such they may have to go. Once the birds are gone, there will be little reason to defend the island ecologically, and it will be a short step then to abolishing the human community as it now is in favor of some sort of more "economical scheme." On the other hand, if the island goes over to the otherwise praiseworthy National Gateway Park System, there are plans to eliminate the human community in favor of making the entire island a park. There are perhaps five thousand people living on the island, and it would be an easy matter to pack them all in one Rockaway highrise. A strange housekeeping solution for a community whose only sin for more than a hundred years now is to have sat so lightly upon the area it shared with the egrets and porgies.

IV
The Long Rhythms of the Outer Beach

[De Kooning's] canvases suggest the low, flat landscapes of Long Island: high-keyed pinks and yellows and acid greens, a flicker of noon light, blue heat-haze on the potato fields, a jumble of sun-flushed legs on the sand. . . . The sculptures are a different matter. If the paintings are largely about landscape as body, De Kooning's bronzes are body as landscape. . . . In Clam Digger *De Kooning's love of direct action reaches the outer limits of credibility: this mud-footed golem, clumping along inside his ridged, tormented epidermis, is all gesture, assuming form in a challengingly haphazard way.*

—Robert Hughes
in *Time*

If you sit in the Shinnecock Bait & Tackle, Snack Bar, Tackle, Liquor Bar, Bait during an autumn howler, you may not, even at high noon, be able to see much beyond the neon beer sign suspended inside the window. The full fetch of the nor'easter is driving the spume across the sprawling bar off the jetties and getting everything up in the air. Even here, back of the dune, all the pools on the road are salt water, and that is salt, not grease, upon the windowpane.

"Be careful," says the counter girl, who is curled up back of the space heater reading a Gothic tale. "All the fishermen around here have their pickups rot out in a year."

"I've got to remember this time to watch it when I step out the back door," says the bartender. "I always think the back door is safe, but the truth is that it's apt to be a good deal deeper than the front." He looks at the tide chart next to the drink list. "And it's going to be after dark when I'll be making my move home."

What makes the back door deeper than the front is Shinnecock Bay, first of a series of wide, shallow bodies of water that run down the South Shore of Long Island from here at Shinnecock, thirty-five miles west of Montauk, all the way to Coney Island at the

39

southeast corner of New York harbor. The Jersey beach, which forms a right angle with Long Island, protects a similar series of bays from Sandy Hook to Cape May.

Outside the building, visible between gusts, are the bottom struts of a Coast Guard tower rising high above the inlet, a structure so solitary that the Coast Guard has abandoned the watch. The first time I saw it, we had been running a ketch close to the beach in order to reduce a potential compass error before plunging off into the gloom for Barnegat Light Ship, and had hit the sand bar which spread well beyond the charted distance.

Wallowing in the rip, our keel bouncing off that sand a dozen times, all kettles and cats adrift, we had looked up to see that tower. It seemed all there was of the land. Because we thought it was inhabited by a watchman, we used the radio, but the cracked voice which represented our hope assured us he was not the eye of God high in the tower, but an adolescent housed in a new station that was located inland from the barrier beach, among the hedges of mansions and country clubs.

It was just as well; we chinned out on our main boom, careened our keel enough to spring it free, and, with our feet dragging in the roiling sand, crawled off into our proper seaborne solitude.

Later I got to ride a small plane down to the Hackensack Meadows to photograph the phragmites and thus show the state of New Jersey what would happen if they put the football Giants there. On our way we swung along the outer beach from Montauk. Beneath the water we saw the outer bar running parallel to the beach. Whales sometimes got caught there, and there was a whale fishery using surfboats that went back in time to the Shinnecock Indians, boats out of which had evolved the harpooning techniques of the offshore men of Melville's days. Whales were caught commercially off Amagansett until 1918. The most famous of them is the fifty-seven-foot right whale captured on Washington's Birthday 1907 by several boat crews under sail and oar. Seventy-eight-year-old Captain Josh Edwards did the lancing and the ironing, and Roy Chapman Andrews later salvaged and reassembled the skeleton which is still the featured exhibition in the American Museum of Natural History.

Bleeding out from the shore we saw not the blood of right whales, but red patches of garnet sand and, on the bluffs, potato fields right to the very edge of the sea. We saw boats trolling for blues and, two miles away, the schools they were after, their feeding tearing the surface like an infection. Farther on, an otter trawl was setting its doors for bottom fish, the big boards slicing away to spread the net as it sank. A few miles down, some men were setting a seine net for top feeders, using a small boat circling out from the shore. A man was walking his dog, which barked at our shadow. At Jones Beach everyone looked naked, more like the polyps on welcome mats, poignant thought for a god. The tower back at Shinnecock, however, even though seen from this same lordly angle, had lost none of its solitary aspect. Impressive, too, was the sand fanning out from the inlet.

At the other cuts, such as Moriches, the deltas seemed to be primarily inside the breachways, driven there by the sea. Because they were in protected backwaters, these formations grew fragile as flowers. Shinnecock did have such a tidal delta and even some islands marked "the Warners" on the charts, but the chief hydraulic phenomenon was this most undelicate sprawl outside the front door pushing into the very teeth of the Atlantic fetch.

I could not help but be curious about the Shinnecock bar, if for no other reason than that it had almost killed me, and I asked my scientist friend, who was about to barrel-roll us by thrusting his bearlike shoulders, along with a camera, out of the starboard window.

"How could you forget the weekend we spent climbing around on all that junk at Montauk?" he said. "There's your answer."

If you climb around under the lighthouse at Montauk, you can indeed find the answer. There, after scrambling over various hard objects all day in search of blow holes into which you might cast for bass, you become aware that some of the hard objects are not rocks but pieces of concrete, and those things you've been grabbing, or that have been grabbing you, are reinforcing rods. Up above, part of the wall still dangles, and there, seeming to lean out over you, is the great tower itself. The littoral current has been moving the ends of the island westward. It used to have a free run along two-thirds of the length of the island before it was intercepted by the pattern off Fire Island Inlet. Since the famous 1938 hurricane, however, there has been a breachway at Shinnecock and one a little farther at Moriches. The current pushing out from these jetties and the jetties themselves have caused the riverlike littoral current to drop much of its load earlier.

It would seem at first that since the prevailing wind is southwest, the littoral would move from New York harbor east toward Montauk, but this is a summer sailor's view which ignores the heavier nor'easters and their unlimited fetch in from the Aran Islands. The warmer and therefore lighter sou'westers have their fetch mitigated by the Jersey coast.

Flying down the South Shore until you come into the Kennedy flight pattern over Jamaica Bay, you can see these inlets repeated a half-dozen times. Looking down toward Fire Island Light, you can see some four miles of sand between it and the inlet at the edge of which it was built in 1857. There are places on the map called "old inlet" right in the middle of long, sandy stretches, and inlets like Moriches and Shinnecock that have been knocked through in my lifetime. Although the littoral is reversed from west to east, the same thing is happening along the Jersey shore, most famously at Barnegat and Sandy Hook, and most recently at Cape May.

Not only does the sea move the sand laterally, but it also moves it in and out. In fact, much of the sand that the littoral has to spend along the beach comes from the withdrawing phase of this in-and-out process. Late in the year the winds are cold, making the waves heavy and steep so that they hit deeper into the beach in places where the summer waves have not reached to flatten and pack the sand. The berm, this soft, vulnerable pile, lies just before the dunes.

The winter seas hit into this abrupt mound and, as happens whenever water hits an obstacle, the force increases. Turbulence way in excess of that of the summer seas carries much greater amounts of sand away until the water deepens and the turbulence slows, dropping the load and forming the winter bar. By the end of the winter these outer bars are at their steepest, and they break up the heavy waves which built the bar in the first place. The waves which then reach the shore are gentler, and these begin rebuilding the beach by carrying in the winter bar, moving only up the gentler slope of the beach, pushing the winter bar before them and retreating slowly, much of the energy sinking into the sand as each wave withdraws so that little sand is carried out with it. The berm begins to build again. The exchange between berm and bar, however, does not balance out. A few major winter storms can put more sand into the sea than can be returned by the summer process, which by definition cannot put forth extra effort to make up for the excess of a particular winter. Furthermore, sand on the bar is picked up by the littoral and moved not in but down the beach, so that while the sand is not lost to the over-all system, it is lost locally. Something old is gone; something new is born.

Understanding how beaches are made and remade is essential not only to mariners but to anyone trying to preserve the ecology. As Stephen Davenport has said in *The New York Times Magazine,* "Nature has never made a permanent beach, and she never will. For a beach is *supposed* to move. It is *supposed* to change its shape, thinning out or disappearing altogether in one spot and perhaps gradually reappearing someplace else."

It is exactly this fact—that nothing is really lost in the over-all system—that makes the problem of beach conservation so interesting philosophically. Davenport quotes Frank Panuzio, senior consulting engineer of the Corps of Engineers, as saying, "You have to think of it [Long Island South Shore] as all one beach, because that's what it is; and you have to treat it consistently. At the very least you have to be consistent from inlet to inlet. Put a jetty in or a group of jetties to hold the sand in one place, and though the sand is likely to build up on the updrift side, you are robbing from the downdrift beach. The beach doesn't know anything about the political boundaries between towns, and a private beach doesn't know it's private."

And yet, included in the platform of local candidates up and down the stretch of outer beach from Montauk to Cape May, right up there along with something about the automobile traffic, the excessive congregation of teen-agers, and the newest monster port or bridge, will be something about "stabilizing the inlet." The proposal puts one in mind of the new Coast Guard engineering unit located in Long Island Sound which has as its announced goal "taking the fear out of the sea."

Stepping out the back door of Shinnecock Bait at low tide, in daylight, seems like a good idea. It is clearly better than trying to force the front door into the storm, and it is also superior to waiting until darkness, when any door will betray you. Even so, a few yards off the stoop there is trouble, and if you've left your boots in the truck out of politeness, you must now be prepared to pitter-patter, leap, and heel-strut your way through all manner of puddles to a narrow pier.

This wobbling structure is not only awash with bay; it is encumbered by a crew of bass fishermen, who at dawn had prepared to face the ocean but had now retreated with all their sweaters, waders, plug bags, and hoods to a place traditionally reserved for the very old, very young, or very poor—for those who drop cheap hand lines for porgy and flounder. It is an awkward position for men who have so heavily invested in the outer beach. No longer the high-arcing cast that defies the very width of the Atlantic. Instead the fierce casting plugs are all in the bags, and the poles, in order that they might drop clams close to the spile, are held as close to the knees as possible while the superfluous ten feet or so of reel and butt sticks out behind the fishermen in a constant embarrassment of ignominious clattering and coupling.

Awkward as their method is, it has produced buckets full of six- to eight-pound blackfish, or what the Indians called tautog. Although good tasting, the fish lacks the hard beauty of the blue or bass, those virile chasers of other fish in swift current and surf. The blackfish has rather the soft ugliness of the bottom feeder, of a sipper of things dropped, or at best a muncher of things stuck. To aid in consuming this menu, the blackfish is equipped with tiny lips full of big, sharp teeth and an anus which is used to turn out shrapnel made from the partially digested shells of green crabs, snails, oysters, and even small lobsters. I used to find eight-pounders in my lobster pots in Connecticut. At Shinnecock these blackfish, usually found out over the oyster and clam beds in the bay or along the rocks in the breachway, had evidently been confused by the silting and smashing of the storm. The more snails to be found along the pier spiles were what they could, at the moment, depend on for food.

Whether or not the silt remains in the beds for a long time is always the question. On the New London–Orient Point ferry I'd been lucky enough to meet two South Shore watermen who had come over to Wilcox's fishing supply house in Stonington, Connecticut, to buy an otter trawl net in order to replace their income during a shellfish layoff at Blue Point down on Great South Bay. The layoff had not been occasioned by silting, however, but by conditions in an area that had little ecological connection with Long Island. On the north shore of Cape Cod there had been a red tide that summer, and the resulting consumer panic had also shut down the buying at Blue Point, where there was no red tide. A similar panic had occurred, the watermen explained, a few years earlier when Mx, a virus different from red tide but no less deadly, had hit the Chesapeake Bay crop.

"People should understand that our area is unique," one of the watermen had said. "The Chesapeake has all those industrial towns dumping into it, and after heavy rains in the mountains the rivers really put out with bad stuff. The Long Island bays have no river like that. In Massachusetts, on the other hand, they are more open to the sea, so that, should a virus like red tide hit, it's going to be damned hard to close off the beds. With our inlets, though, and the strong littoral moving across the mouths, most of the sea can go right on past."

A storm like this can change things radically in the breachway, too. Bass holes open and close like hamburger joints on the urban strip. A skin diver came along the pier, flippers in hand, face sadder than the pressure of his wet suit would ordinarily allow. "A day like this and I can lose my fifty-foot hole," he said. I asked him what was in his fifty-foot hole, and he said sadly, "Porgies, bass, blacks, mackerel, fluke, flounder, sharks."

"That's some hole," I said.

"One guy got a two-hundred-forty-pound sunfish," he said.

To stabilize fishing off the beach, the Shinnecock Fishermen's Association is planning to dump some junk cars out there and thus become the Shinnecock Reef Fishermen's Association.

In the alleys between head-high stacks of lobster pots danced small spirals of what I had at first thought was some sort of tumbling beach weed, a bit too tropical in its transparent hue. I picked it up to find it was monofilament, no doubt cut off by fishermen whose rigs had been nicked by the rocks. Mixed in with tumbling monofilament, the puddles, and the shadows of sea gulls was another series of wings, these stacked like bats

Beacon Falls · **Wallingford** ⊚   ○ East Haddam   ○ Montville ⊚   ○ Ledyard   ⊚ Potter

○ Bethany   ○ Quinnipiac   Tylerville ○   Chesterfield ○   Uncasville ⊚ ○ Gales Ferry   North Stonington ○   White Rock

Hamden ⊚   N. Haven ○ Northford   Chester ○·   Hadlyme ○   Quaker Hill   Conning Towers   ○ Old Mystic   Pawcatuck ⊕ ⊚ Westerl

○ Augerville   Clintonville   Deep River ○   ○ Hamburg   **New** ⊚ ⊚ Groton   **West Mystic**

Woodbridge ○ Whitneyville   ○ Montowese   Ivoryton ○   East Lyme ○   **London**   Morningside Pk. ⊚ Mystic ○ Stonington

○ N. Guilford   Centerbrook ○ Essex   Niantic ○   Poquonock Bridge   Avondale

New Haven   ○ Foxon   ○ North Branford   Old Lyme ○   Crescent Beach   Pleasure   Noank   Misquamic

Allingtown ○   Guilford   East River   Old Saybrook   S. Lyme ○   Beach   Groton Long Point   Watch Hill

○ Orange   **East Haven**   Branford ○   Madison ⊕ Clinton   Saybrook Point   Sound View

West Haven ○   Stony Creek ○   Westbrook   Fishers Island

Woodmont ○   Momauguin   Leetes Island   Grove Beach

d   Short Beach   Pine Orchard

on

G   I S L A N D   S O U N D   Block Island Sound

G   ○ Plum Island

     East Marion ○   Orient ○   Gardiners Island

     Greenport ⊕   Gardiners Bay   Gardiners Island

     Shelter Island Hts.   Dering Harbor

     Southold ○   Shelter Island   Montauk ○

     Peconic ○   Montauk Lighthouse

     Cutchogue ○   N Haven ○   Springs ○

Belle Terre ○ Sound Beach   Mattituck ⊕   New Suffolk   ○ Noyack   Sag Harbor   ⊕ Amagansett   Napeague Beach

Port Jefferson   ○ Shoreham   Northville   Laurel ○   Little Peconic Bay   Freetown ⊕   East Hampton

○ Miller Place   ○ Wading River   Aquebogue ○   Jamesport   Bridgehampton ⊕   ○ Wainscott

○ Mount Sinai   Rocky   ○ Wading River Sta.   S. Jamesport ○   Great   Sagaponcka ○

etauket   Point   **Riverhead** ⊚.   Peconic Bay   Water Mill ○

bor   Terryville   ○ Calverton   Flanders ○   Shinnecock Hills

○ Middle   ○ Ridge   Southampton ⊕

each ○ Selden   Island   ○ Upton   ○ Manorville   Hampton Bays ○   ⊕ Southampton

○ Coram   Shinnecock Bay

rove   **SUFFOLK**   ○ Yaphank   Speonk ○   East Quogue ○

nkonkoma   ○ Farmingville   E. Moriches   Eastport   Westhampton

ook ○ Medford   Holtsville   Moriches ○   Quogue ⊙

e Highlands   Mastic-Shirley ⊕   Center Moriches   Remsenburg   **Westhampton Beach**

Patchogue ⊚   Brookhaven ○   Mastic   Moriches Bay

oint   E. Patchogue ⊙ Bellport ○   Beach ⊕

○ Bayport

yville   Great South Beach

st Sayville   **LONG ISLAND**

        ATLANTIC OCEAN

trying out for a totem pole. I looked up and saw they were swordfish tails fastened to a spile. They looked rather old, even older than last July when they might have been caught noon-dozing some twenty-five miles south of here. Around on the other side of a stack of pots a man was looking out to where a boat with a tuna tower and pulpit was riding at the pier. He had on one of those long-billed hats that keep off the sun when you're up in the tower craning around, trying to tell a flopping dorsal fin from one that runs straight. It turned out it was his boat, his tails.

"Oh, sure, I still chase a few around, mercury or no mercury. In fact this mercury business has been good for them, maybe give them a chance to come back. The Foreign Nationals been getting them all with those long lines. Rigs like that take not only the old dozers up in the sun, but the young ones, too. I set a line once myself, just a couple of miles, and hell, we caught ones the size of a ball bat and half et up by dogfish at that. It was a slaughter. I never set one again, but that don't stop them Foreign Nationals. They'll set anything and take everything until we might as well go drive the beer truck."

"The rain has let up and the sun shines brightly through a haze that must be made, at least in part, of sea spume. For some reasons, now that it has cleared, the foghorn has come on, a sharp peep that sets your teeth on edge."

I wrote this later, sitting in the safety of the truck. I had my boots on and so felt a bit cockier than I had earlier when stepping about back by the docks. After a morning of backwatering and barring I was also a little too anxious to get out onto the beach itself. Like a kid with new boots dashing into the year's first snow, I jumped down from the steep winter berm which had already formed here this year and began to trot along the narrow beach that was left. The fifth—or was it the ninth?—wave caught me, hit my heel, and rolled right up my calf and over the back of my knee. This seemed very unfair to me, for the water moving across the beach had not been more than a few inches deep. Then I remembered how a sea will come in rather flatly to a lighthouse, hit quietly, and then come to life, climbing straight up, hand over hand, sometimes to the very top.

Once I had gotten wet, I decided I might as well continue along what beach there was. Something was tumbling in front of me—mustaches, it looked like, cat mustaches tweaked out for twirling by Salvador Dali. Four or five of them, skidding and tumbling ahead. I caught up with one. It was a skate sac. Some American skates get to be four feet long, but these egg pouches looked rigged for the more common size one usually finds in a lobsterman's bait barrel, a tough fish good to mix in with softer flats and herring to give some permanence to the string.

In the edge of the breaking wave was a series of strange shapes like the bones of a ship. When I got up next to it, however, I saw how the pattern resembled the fish trap the Patchogue watermen had shown me on the ferryboat.

This kind of trap takes advantage of the fact that the fish, mainly bass or blue, will at some time during the day move along the shore within six hundred feet of the beach, feeding in the littoral and surf. To catch them you need two things: something to guide them and something to hold them. To guide them the fishermen build a six-hundred-foot fence of stakes and net straight out from the beach. Near the end they construct two wing fences that funnel in the fish as they move out along the straight fence, seeking a way around it. At the end of this funnel a second one leads into a twenty-foot-square box with an open top. At two openings, then, the fish have been presented with a wide area to get in but, once in, with only a narrow way out. The more fish there are inside, the greater the panic, and the less chance there is that they will find a way out. When the fisherman makes his rounds, he merely hoists the floor of the twenty-foot box. It is rigged to tilt toward him, and soon the fish all come tumbling to his gaff.

A closer look at the stakes revealed that they had not so much weathered into those weird shapes as merely grown into them, for they were made of twisted scrub oak, virtually raw from the woods, side limbs crudely lopped. I remembered that when I'd asked the two Patchogue watermen what they paid for their lumber they had sheepishly said, "The woods." Somebody, of course, owns all the land on Long Island, yet it is still possible for a man who knows how to use a resource like the sea to employ land not, strictly speaking, his own, though I doubt that even fishermen these days can duplicate what the old oysterman I once worked with did. Most of his sloop was built in and of the Long Island woods. One day in 1880 he had simply moved with his ax, hammer, and adze in among the trees (not his own) and stayed there until it was time to call some friends who owned a pair of oxen to haul the hull out.

I watched the seas break in through the fish trap. There were no boulders along the whole beach except for the ones in the box. Dozens of waves must have rattled those rocks before I realized something significant. The wings and box were, after all, right at the edge of the water, and the berm was at my back. Where was the six hundred feet of fence between the water's edge and the trap itself? Even allowing for the fact that my watermen had been working the shallow bay, this ocean model must have had a lead-in at least half as long as that they'd sketched. Could this beach have advanced two hundred feet since the trap was built? It was impossible to judge how old the trap was because of the nature of the wood, and yet I wondered: how long would such stakes stand up?

Out beyond the trap the cross seas on the bar were beginning to catch fire with the autumn afternoon sun. There was already a good deal of amber in them from the sand. I set sail in my pickup down the beach road. It no longer was macadam shining with a thin layer of rain, but a channel quivering with a load of wind-blown water. To the right, Shinnecock and Moriches bays had seeped past the outer guard of duck blinds, up through yellowing spartina grass and red pickleweed, past the wet blond phragmites and around the final sentry line of telephone poles, and as I headed west for Patchogue I imagined I was boom out in one of the grand thirty-five-foot gaff catboats of the late famous Patchogue shipbuilder Samuel Wicks. Plumb bowed, we'd be, with a heart-shaped transom raked like the sterns of pilot schooners. A gust came in over the dunes, and I was glad Miriam Wicks had put four sets of reef points in the mainsail and that I had lashed my oyster tongs inside the cockpit.

Cape May Point

Cape May: Ocean-front boarding houses
and (opposite) a view of the beach

Fishing boat in Jarvis Sound, Wildwood Crest

Cape May harbor

Along the Maurice River near Leesburg

Looking across the Maurice River toward Bivalve

Pleasure boats docked in the
Cohansey River near Greenwich

Woods along Muskee Creek

Marsh near Heislerville

Autumn color along West Creek
not far from Delmont—

—and in a Cape May
Courthouse marsh

Brigantine Beach

Pier at Brigantine

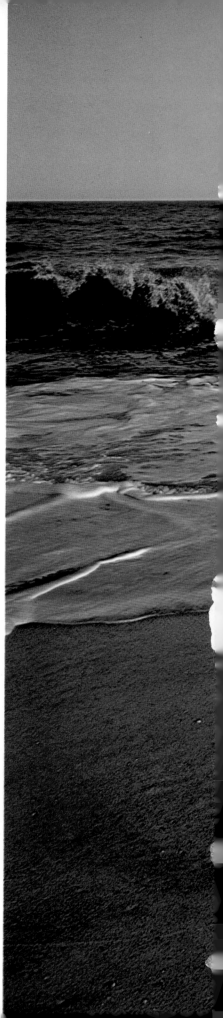

Sand and surf, South Jersey

Snowy egret, Little Egg Harbor

Wetlands below Tuckerton

Great Bay

Brigantine National Wildlife Refuge

Crabbing, Barnegat

Pine barrens, Wharton State Forest

The Mullica River

Toms River tributary

Grasses in a cedar swamp near Toms River

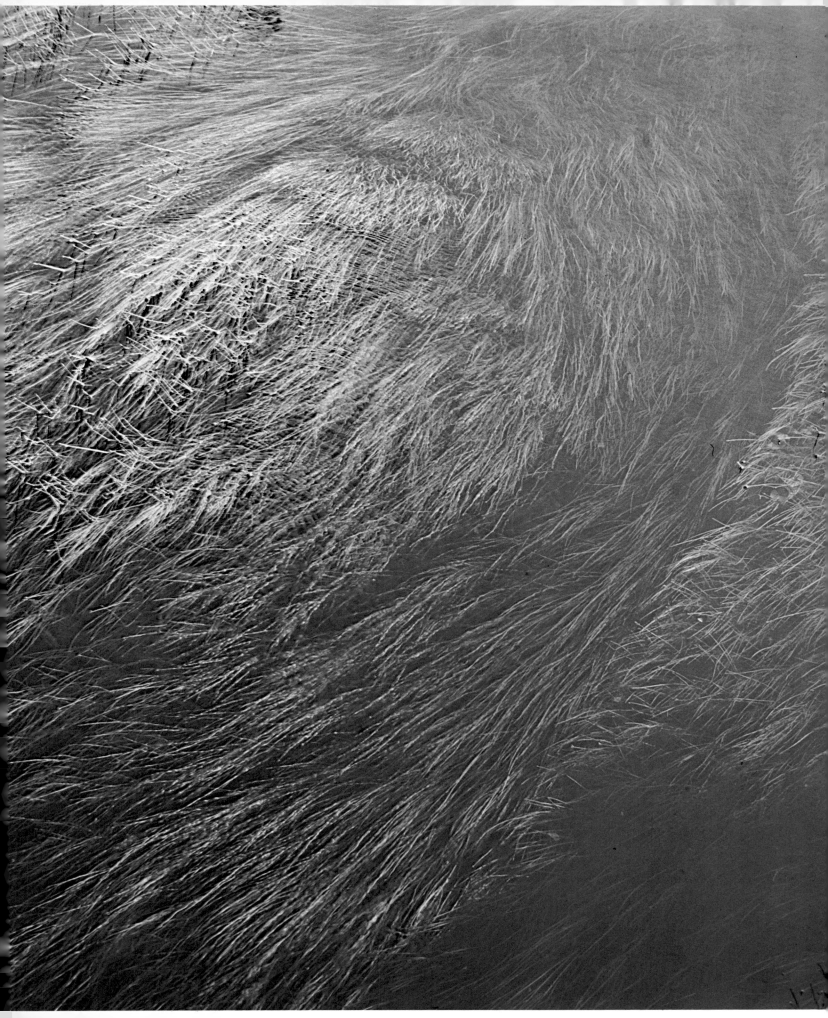

Tide ripples, a horseshoe crab, and marsh grasses in Sandy Hook State Park

RIGHT: Digging clams at Sandy Hook against a backdrop of the Navesink Highlands

OVERLEAF: The New York skyline from Caven Point, Jersey City

New York harbor, looking toward Staten Island

Gowanus Canal Basin, Brooklyn

Tug off Staten Island

Manhattan's East River Drive

The *Nieuw Amsterdam* leaving New York

Tug and tow passing beneath Brooklyn Bridge

Exploring the Jamaica Bay Wildlife Sanctuary

Jones Beach

Oak Island, Great South Bay

Surf casting, Robert Moses State Park, Fire Island

Scenes in the Bayard Cutting Arboretum, Great River

Dune grasses

Shinnecock Bay, "first of a series of wide, shallow bodies of water . . ."

". . . a beach is *supposed* to move "

Dunes, Amagansett

Autumn sunset, Shinnecock Bay

"Potato fields right to the very edge of
the sea" in Mecox (right) and Wainscott

Beach house, Bridgehampton

Beach, Southampton

Duck pond, Bridgehampton

Looking out "over the ceaseless roll of the Atlantic "

Fishing boat off Promised Land in Gardiners Bay

Kellis Pond, Bridgehampton

Hook Pond, East Hampton

Street in East Hampton

In East Hampton

Napeague harbor

OVERLEAF: View across Block Island Sound, looking toward the Connecticut shore

Montauk Point

Montauk Light

V
Equipment

Although we ourselves were formed by imperceptible growth,
we do not know how to create anything in that way . . . and are
unable to visualize a movement so slow that a perceptible result
springs from an imperceptible change. We can imagine the
living process only by lending it a rhythm which is specifically
ours and has no connection with what happens in the creature
we are observing.

—Paul Valéry
"Man and the Sea Shell"

A beach, of course, can be a lovely thing, but that fall the engine in the boat had not proved reliable. As we went for bass and blues along the Rhode Island shore, it frequently hiccuped itself into minor coronaries during such major events as trolling atop the third wave out from the sand. One afternoon I noticed figures on the shore. Although I was spending most of my time diving into the engine hatch and then rushing up to spin the wheel toward the open sea, there was a moment when I checked the distance to the beach and there they were.

At first I thought they were some vestige of the old Rhode Island wreckers come to bludgeon us in the undertow. Their gear, however, seemed much too frail for skulls like ours, and the lines that spun out from their poles made elegant trajectories. There was also an enviable stability to their performance. Whereas we were constantly skating across the wet cockpit into each other's gear, they stood firmly, implacably apart from each other. As we fumbled our lines and bead chains off the stern, there they were casting like trout fishermen, and as we scrambled out to sea, jerking and cranking, there they stood in their idyllic bower.

And some of their poles were bent.

We used to carry our equipment to the boat in a red jeep. It was old enough to be nearly floorless, and its canvas top was mildewed. I did not think of it so much as a car as an unusually large, strong wheelbarrow, one with a reliable engine. Safely ashore, we listened to that engine.

"Those bent poles today," I said. "Those guys had fish."

"Those guys we saw today had jeeps," said Holcomb.

"It's O.K., skipper," said Vole, and he put his oilskinned arm around me. "Next time we just won't get in quite so close."

"You don't understand," said Holcomb. "That's where the fish were. Jeeps. All we'd have to do is slap on three rod holders, right on the front bumper."

"You mean drive along the sand in the car after fish?" I said.

"Not at all," said Holcomb. "The whole thing is being in the right place at the right time with the right equipment. I know where we can get the pipe, and for the bumper I've got a drill and I've got a metal bit that will fit perfect."

A week later we drove along the same beach, chasing sandpipers and spotting an occasional brace of terns. The terns twittered and looped spastically before they plunged into their meals. The jeep's engine roared. Through the holed floor sand boiled up and the mildewed top tested our heads. The surf poles, newly acquired, trembled in Holcomb's holders and our casting plugs danced out free from the guides to swing like drunken windshield wipers. In the sea beneath the terns, however, lurked nothing we could fascinate.

But we were not entirely alone. In summer, of course, these beaches are thick with towels and flesh, and the air is heavy with the cries of children, the top ten tunes, and the left-field wall at Fenway Park. Now there were only other beach buggies, one every mile or so and in challenging variety: a blue jeep, topless, with a whip aerial tucked down as if ready for an epic *thwong;* a green panel truck with rusted body, faded lettering: PER-GOLOSSI'S BAKERY; an old De Soto with half-flat tires. We waved to all of these as in the old days you used to wave to boats. Most waved back. Slowly.

"Hey," called the man in the bread truck, "don't chase terns. Just chase gulls."

We plowed to a stop and peered through the slowing swing of our casting plugs toward the actual sea. It looked awfully big. Fortunately there were things out there holding it down, the U.S.S. *Skylark* for one, an ocean-going rescue tug that the Navy used for training divers. Its gray hull was relieved by two giant orange diving buoys hung in the superstructure. Beyond the *Skylark* were two thick gray lines. The one on the left was Block Island, on the right Montauk Point. "That's where the fish are," said the man in the blue jeep with the aerial.

In the sky, three football fields down the beach, something twitched. It well might have been a gull. We chased. The sun was setting. We came to where the bird or whatever had been. There was no reason it couldn't have been a gull, and so, though it was no longer there, we jumped out, yanked our poles from the holders—knights selecting a lance—and charged the sea.

The water was warm around our knee boots, and even when it slopped over the top, it still was warm. I kept walking out into the sea, and my faith was rewarded. The water got shallower. I was mounting the bar. It was as if I'd gotten some sort of extension on my credit, and I wondered if I might not just keep going like that, through recession and recovery, all the way out past the *Skylark* to Montauk. I decided, however, to accept what I had, stood my ground, and cast. Amazingly I got my plug back every time.

We sat on the hood of the jeep and ate supper. Vole, who had been the cook aboard the boat, could not help gathering things. This time it was an injured sanderling, and, in the nest of Vole's hands, it looked like a brother thumb. The *Skylark* held the last of the day on its orange diving buoys. The sanderling peeped. Montauk Light came on.

The bird peeped.

At dusk there were shapes coming out of the dunes—nuns, brown and black ones, floating over the brown sand that was going black—brown and black nuns spilling out from the dunes, through the snow fence from their convent beyond the tall grass. Their feathered habits trailed soundlessly. Some seemed headed for the sea as if to test the soundlessness of their clothing in the surf.

"Montauk's the place to be," said Holcomb. His face was full of cheese, meat loaf, and bread, and as he chewed, his red goatee rose and fell neatly as a hydraulic press. "There can be no doubt about it, this place has had it."

"Nighttime," came a voice from the bread truck. "Change your lures."

"To hell with that," said Holcomb, "let's change our ground."

There was a way to change our ground, to get to Montauk without having to walk out into the water. It was, after all, only the longer tail of that island which old natives like the Indians and Walt Whitman called Paumanok, or fish-shaped, and which later, less visual, perhaps more weary inhabitants called Long Island. The head of the fish was a hundred miles west of Montauk, shoved up into New York harbor in the form of Brooklyn. The island could always be boarded at that end by a variety of spans, the most salty of which was Hart Crane's Brooklyn Bridge whose "cables breathe the North Atlantic still."

Another way, closer at hand and a good deal saltier, was the ferryboat from New London to Orient Point, the shorter, near tail fin of the fish. The two tails, Montauk and Orient Point, composed nearly one third of the fish. In the water that lay between them— Great Peconic Bay, Little Peconic, and Gardiners Bay—were the attendant islands of Shelter and Gardiners. To get from Orient to Montauk one could drive all the way up to the middle of the tail at Riverhead, or cut across from tip to tip by means of the ferries that ran from Greenport to Shelter Island and from there to the old whaling port of Sag Harbor. To take the curse off the driving then, we chose the Shelter Island route. Added to the first ferry, this gave us three boats in all.

The first ferry, we discovered, was a delightful old World-War-II-Is-Fun landing barge, a big, gray shoebox of a ship that opened its end late one cold afternoon in New London harbor and swallowed our jeep. Chains rattled and crewmen shouted in the hollow iron enclosure. The ramp lifted to close behind us—all vassals and fair maidens within the keep. All dragons and heavy seas, we hoped, without.

We climbed through a haze of diesel onto the upper deck and into a northeast wind anticipating winter. Off the mouth of the river, beyond the lighthouse whose oscillations between light and dark figure so heavily in the brooding background of Eugene O'Neill's meditations on the local character, the New York islands stood out in autumn clarity. Rock and sand put together in various sizes, these islands formed the second stage of the terminal moraine that reaches from Orient Point on across to the Connecticut–Rhode Island border at Watch Hill. Presently used for bird sanctuaries, animal disease laboratories, lighthouses, and, in the case of Fishers Island, a small number of large homes, the islands seemed ready to take off straight up from their sea beds. Plum, Great Gull, Little Gull, Fishers, South Dumpling, North Dumpling, Flat Hammock, Sea Flower . . . all ready to go. There were holes in Fishers which made it seem as if there were even more islands, and its far end looked as if it had been pried loose from the water by a spatula.

We leaned on the gray iron rail as the bow shuddered into the rip at the river mouth, where the offshore seas hit the flood tide and the wind moaned in the old bolt holes where antiaircraft guns had been fixed for that other war.

A few small boats were in the lee of the lighthouse—a big, square building that looked more than ever like an apartment broken loose from New London. A week earlier a man fishing for mackerel on a six-pound test line had caught a twelve-pound bluefish. There was a ledge on the south side of the light where at low tide you might hook a fat bass or two. Past the ledge, out toward Bartletts Reef, a man in a Nova-Scotia-type lobster boat was skidding away from us down a following sea as he headed west for Niantic. His long, low cockpit was piled high with lobster pots coming in for the winter. When the flat stern of the boat got caught on a crest, it looked as if the whole season were pursuing him, about to topple and break him like the fishermen in Hokusai's "The Great Wave." The spindle marking Bartletts erupted every third wave. In spite of Holcomb's request that the trip remain purely a sporting encounter, I couldn't help but recall how the winter before an oil spill had taken place out there, a barge-load of light-grade oil that had spread quickly for miles along the Sound.

The sun grew redder and rounder as it prepared to sink in the waters down toward New York City, and I listened to the wind moan through the old machine-gun holes and wondered just whose bread and butter this stretch of sea and land was. Holcomb, in spite of his earlier remark about keeping the trip pure, was frowning.

"What is it?" I said.

"That's it," said Holcomb. "I don't even know. What the hell, I use all that stuff, and I know the Russians have submarines that run right up this Sound, but it's all going to be gone, the fish and the birds, and it's all going to be like down New York City way, and I don't want to move." He looked wildly around, as if maybe there were some sort of parapet, some higher turret he could climb into in order to fight the battle better, but we were already up where it was mostly wind, and what steel we had was cold and rusty. The land no longer protected us from the seas, and the blunt bow that had once opened to send forth the bayoneted rifles of invasion banged square into a sea, and the spray sailed up to involve us. We ducked and heard it rattle down upon the hoods of the semis in the hold. Behind the windshield of a snappy hardtop, a well-dressed man looked up from his newspaper with alarm.

"Oh, oh," said Vole, and he looked down at the man in the hardtop. "Another customer just made for the highway bridge."

"Vole," said Holcomb, "you're really out to ruin my fishing trip."

116

Greenport is the railhead for the North Shore, an old shellfish town indeed at the end of the line. She had known glory not only from fish but from that other great maritime activity, rum-running. In Prohibition her position gave her quick access to New York City and a number of back bays. The end of Prohibition, coinciding as it did with the Depression, plus an eel-grass blight that affected the entire aquatic food chain, and finally the 1938 hurricane (which put the boats in the streets), introduced a series of disasters from which the town is just now recovering. Greenport is home to a large fishing fleet that pursues with seine nets the menhaden, which, as at Cape May, congregate in tremendous schools. The fish are taken to nearby Promised Land, where there is a plant that renders them into meal. There is also a shellfish factory where clams and oysters are opened and then repacked in containers humans can better understand.

Since we were going to cook our own meals, we had to stop at the store. Vole is painfully particular about his selections, so Holcomb and I gave him some money and left him to it and took ourselves into a bar. There was one old customer inside. He mumbled something about scallops. The bartender explained that the old man's boat was down at the wharf, but the sheriff had slapped a plaster on it. The old man said he was going fishing.

"For scallops?" said Holcomb.

The old man looked at him.

"Fishing for scallops," said Holcomb, and he tried turning his hand into what he understood to be the unique manner in which a scallop would manage itself.

"No more," said the fisherman as he watched Holcomb's hand. "No," he said at last, "no more."

Vole came out of the store with his arms full of brown bags, a long string of sausages hung around his neck like ammunition for Pancho Villa. We stowed the gear, and Vole said we should find the scalloper's boat. Back of the store were wharfs and fishing boats, small wooden trawlers. There was one that was lower than the others, a catboat of extraordinarily low freeboard, its sheer as delicate as a Staffordshire tea saucer. The mast, however, was sawed off six feet up, and an engine filled the cockpit. Tacked on the rounded corner of the oversize cabin was a sign with large block lettering. In the dark it was hard to read, but there was enough light for us to know that the boat was enjoined not to leave the pier and that the penalties were severe.

"No more scallops," I said.

We drove down to the wharf where the ferry would take us to Shelter Island. The boat was halfway across. We waited by a hotel with fake brick siding, a peeling veranda, and men on the steps who looked as though they might be in training to take the old scalloper's place.

From the ferry gate ambled a big fellow costumed like a railroad man, in denim coveralls, cap, steel-rimmed eyeglasses. He swung open the picket gate. The bow of the ferry was smacking the spiles. There was room for a half-dozen cars. We drove on alone.

Although the waters of Peconic Bay did not seem as vast as those we had crossed to reach Orient Point, the smaller size of the boat, the darkness, and the mood set by the old scalloper and the asbestos hotel combined to make us aware of the maritime uncertainties, and we felt as if we were no longer on an automobile trip. Out there in the gloom, for

117

instance, we knew was Gardiners Island, and off it the Ruins, an 1812 fort used even now for bomb runs but known to us as an alternate hole for blues early in the season. There was an even better spot around from the Ruins at a place called Cherry Harbor, just out from the windmill on Gardiners.

Unlike most places where bluefishing is good, the Cherry Harbor range was not uncomfortable water, and we'd once had a delightful day trolling beneath the windmill. The usual mob of two hundred or so high-powered maniacs who charged about to outfish their neighbors in The Race had been absent. Instead we had had less than a dozen boats, each respectful of the other's interest. There, for one, was a man from Mystic—boots up, boom out—trailing a line from the transom of his ninety-year-old Crosby catboat and making a slightly rumpled version of Currier & Ives's classic "Trolling for Blues." There, too, was the launch *Ol' Blue* with the research crew from the University of Noank Marine Laboratory.

They were using a small gill net, and if we thought a bluefish could be mean coming up off a forty-pound test line, we were even more impressed by the difficulties the men on the launch were having with what was thrashing over their gunwale, raw off a relatively cozy fight. Vole had once been bitten to the bone by a fish that had been ten minutes in the cockpit. All the blood had drained from his face. It had taken six stitches to sew up his hand. Everyone in the village has a favorite bluefish atrocity story, and so it was with much interest that we had gone down to the laboratory the day the new man on the bluefish-project crew had arrived in his new sports car with lots of stereo equipment, Modigliani repros, and empty Chianti bottles to announce he was going to be "associated with the fisheries survey." In Cherry Harbor that day he was having his premier association, for it was his job to remove the fish from the net and hold them down for the tagging without benefit of pickax handle, baseball bat, Victorian chair leg, or any of the more orthodox tools the rest of us used to persuade the blue.

He must have done a good job because later reports were coming in telling of tagged fish showing up all along the Atlantic coast. Bluefish, the scientists learned, have, like wine and college football teams, vintage and lean years that seem to run in cycles. Just what all the determining factors are remains difficult to assess at present because the ocean is hardly a controlled laboratory, but one thing seems true: a strong year's crop can put up with more than a weak one, so that when one is studying the effects of certain environmental changes, one must be careful about the ages of fish found "unaffected." There might still be fish after an environmental disaster, and they might be as big as ever, but there could also be whole generations wiped out, so that when the hardy species had eventually died off, there might be a radical alteration in the population.

Cherry Harbor is an interesting place even if you don't catch fish. It was here Captain Kidd had moored with his topmasts down in 1699 while waiting for the governor of Massachusetts to betray him. Near the end of his stay, Kidd, getting nervous, supposedly buried his treasure ashore. Gardiners Island, however, represents an even greater treasure than a trunkful of European coins, for its 3300 acres of woods and gentle meadows are almost as they were in 1639 when the first Gardiner on the island was awarded the place by Long Island Indians grateful for his assistance against the mainland Narragansetts. Ecologists say that nowhere within a hundred miles of New York City is there another area where they can be as sure about "what outside forces affect the balance of nature of a pure habitat." There are geese, deer, wild turkey and quail, but the most interesting creatures on the island are the ospreys, or fish hawks. As long ago as 1810 John Lyon wrote of these birds that have wing spans as big as a man's outstretched arms:

> *They are sometimes seen high in the air, sailing and cutting strange gambols, with loud vociferations, darting down several hundred yards perpendicular, frequently with part of a fish in one claw, which they seem proud of, and to claim high hook, as the fishermen call him who takes the greatest number.*

The island's ospreys are particularly interesting now as they are practically the only ones of their kind to have escaped the full force of the postwar DDT mania. At a time when osprey nests along the mouth of the Connecticut River and on Long Island itself are empty, Paul Spitzer has found thirty-four young in thirty-eight nests on Gardiners Island. This is a far cry from the 350 nesting pairs on the island in 1945, the last year before spraying, but it is a sign that at least here not all is lost.

In addition to the bass and blues out by Gardiners, Peconic Bay is known for its weakfish, or sea trout, ranking along with such places as Narragansett Bay, Brandywine Shoal in Delaware Bay, Lynnhaven Inlet in the Chesapeake, Indian River on Florida's east coast, and Laguna Madre on the Gulf of Mexico. Weakfish are noted for their mysterious cycles of abundance and scarcity, which some people claim is a function of the bluefish cycle. Others claim it is a function of the menhaden cycle, and still others claim that there is an even larger rhythm which accounts for the cycles of all of these species. In any case, weakfish, plentiful at the time of the American Revolution, became, as Lyman and Woolner have it in *The Complete Book of Weakfish:*

> . . . *so scarce that one, caught off Provincetown . . . in 1838, was sent to Boston for identification—because no fisherman knew what it might have been. Slowly thereafter the supply increased and, from 1901 through 1904, fishing was the best in the history of the new world.*
>
> *Another decline then set in and, by 1910, few were being taken. The fish began to make a comeback in 1921 and increased rather steadily in numbers until 1949, when an abrupt slump occurred. Part of the cause of this may have been an increase in the intensity of the commercial fishery in Chesapeake waters [where one of the groups breeds]. In more recent years there has been a slight gain throughout the northeastern section in such hot spots as Peconic Bay . . . but the catches in 1957 and 1958 could not compare to those of the 1901– 04 era.*

Before we got out to Montauk, there was Shelter Island yet to cross. We drove off the ferry and up through twisting wooded hills past the old inn named for a local Indian tribe. The umbrellaed tables were all put away, and Dering Harbor, which I remembered full as a blooming garden of drying spinnakers, was now empty. My wife and I had once sailed over and rented a bicycle built for two and wobbled along an unpaved road atop a bluff overlooking Peconic Bay, and I now kept an eye out lest we find our jeep involved in just such a spectacular route again.

"Look out," cried Vole.

"What was it?" I said.

"A deer," he said. "Could there be such a thing—a deer?"

"I suppose so," I said and drove even more slowly, catching myself twice reaching for the windshield wipers, as if it were moths I expected to splatter our view.

We waited in the dark by a sign that promised yet another boat. Across the narrow strait there was the ferry itself, a single white boat like the two that ran off Greenport side. It seemed quite happy to be on its side, and we on ours. After all, as Holcomb said, nothing gets real until you are all the way to Montauk, so we sat there, saving up our last island, as it were, breathing the dark autumn air that mingled the falling oak and maple leaves with the salt water.

Eventually one of us realized that the sign warned that no ferry ran after ten. Since it was close to that, we came alive and blinked our lights, not quite daring yet to shatter the mood with a horn bleat.

"Maybe he's waiting for the new bridge," mumbled Holcomb.

"What!" I said. "Is there to be another bridge *here?*"

"There's always got to be another bridge," said Holcomb. "Wake me up when they stop making bridges."

There was a mutter from the diesel across the waters, a metallic unhitching worthy of the Penn Central, and froth uttered forth from under the end of the boat that had chosen this time to be the stern. We watched it slide down current until it seemed it was going around the island and we beeped the horn. It was all part of the ferry's routine, however, and she made her turn, coming back to us, bow against the current.

"It's a good thing," said Holcomb. "I feel like a fool sitting here with the road just coming to an end."

"Then you'll be happy with the new bridge," said Vole.

"I just want to get there," said Holcomb, "and when I get there I don't want there to be a lot of modern stuff that makes it *not being there.*"

Sag Harbor seemed deserted. Even the hollow whale at the foot of the main street seemed a bit glum as we drove past. The place had once been second only to New York as a port of entry and had rivaled Nantucket in whaling, but unlike Greenport the town had retained a prosperous air, thanks to summer people and commuters. We had once blundered onto what was left of a whaling festival in which the whale at the foot of the main street had been rowed about in the harbor chased by young men in whale boats. At night our sun-and-beer headaches had been subjected to a relentless barrage of fireworks managed by John Steinbeck, who had signed announcements to the effect that he was "running scared."

Beyond Sag Harbor it was scrub oak, pine, and darkness. We swept through a town that looked more like White Plains with its wide, well-planted street and careful colonial shopping center. A left turn and we were into darkness again on a two-strip concrete road (a year later tarred over). This was the road built in the 1920s when Montauk was

120

struggling to be invented as, of all things, "The Miami of the North." Before the concrete road was built, there had been only a narrow lane through the strip of sand connecting the point with the fatter part of the island. In fact Montauk was thought of as a kind of island itself, and old-timers spoke of "getting onto it" and "off of it." The Miami visionaries had also built a railroad especially for the fishing business. It was their boast that in 1933 you could leave Brooklyn at 5:30, A.M., and for a dollar and a half get down to Montauk and back. For two dollars there was a boat-and-bait deal and even a refrigerator car for your catch.

Surf casting had been going on, of course, before the invention of Montauk–Miami and the existence of the platforms the developers had poked out into the sea to enable fishermen to get more distance. At least as far back as the nineteenth century men stood under the lighthouse at the very tip of the point and heaved and hauled—that is, slung the line in the manner of David facing Goliath. They employed a heavy tarred line and a lead drail. Thoreau on his trip to Cape Cod reports men fishing this way, and Whitman, who grew up near Montauk, describes his boyhood in the 1830s:

> *round Shelter island, and down to Montauk—spent many an hour on Turtle hill by the old lighthouse, on the extreme point, looking out over the ceaseless roll of the Atlantic. I used to like to go down there and fraternize with the blue-fishers, or the annual squads of sea-bass takers. Sometimes, along Montauk peninsula, (it is some 15 miles long, and good grazing,) met the strange, unkempt, half-barbarous herdsmen, at that time living there entirely aloof from society or civilization, in charge, on those rich pasturages, of vast droves of horses, kine or sheep, own'd by farmers of the eastern towns. Sometimes, too, the few remaining Indians, or half-breeds, at that period left on Montauk peninsula, but now I believe altogether extinct.*

We were riding along the neck leading out to the point itself, a strip of sand and scrub pine along one side of which shone the railroad tracks in the November dew while on either side was the moonlit sea. Holcomb and Vole dozed. Alone on the two strips of 1920 concrete, funneled by the line of telephone poles and rails, I felt more at sea, more remote than I had on the ferries. After all, I thought, hadn't all this been created by the glacier, *terminal* at that, terminal moraine shaped further by *powerful currents?* And this funneling road was obviously designed to go just one way, to draw me inevitably to its end where no ferryboat could save me.

"*I think I'll climb into my tree,*" said a strange voice.

"*What?*" I nearly twisted us off the narrow concrete. "What did you say?" It must have been Vole, for Holcomb had long ago either fallen out of the back or dropped into exile among the grocery bags.

"I think I'll more formally go to sleep," said Vole.

"Oh," I said. For an instant I had really believed he wanted to be left in a tree, a reasonable enough request if one was drowning in what was now all November moonlit sea, and what wasn't sea was sand like snow, or concrete flooded with sand—reasonable enough except there were no longer any trees.

121

We began to rise. Trees did appear. Grass. Up out of the sea bottom we rose and the canvas top flapped. Below us, ahead of us, was not only the sea, but a town, and behind it a harbor big as a lake, and beyond the lake another highland upon which stood a radar tower defending us, its proportions dwarfing telephone poles and trees like a malignant windmill. And there beyond the radar, still small enough so you could block it with your thumb, was the lighthouse—that pin of yearning toward which we had flung our futile rigs that night a month before.

"Well," I said, "here is where the fish are."

"Where?" said Holcomb, rising up out of the grocery bags.

"Right here." I swept the windshield, displaying the town, the lake, the radar, and the light.

What passed under our bow, however, was a rabbit.

We swung down into the town. Vole, with his usual good planning, had already selected the beds upon which we would sleep and the kitchenette in which we would prepare the contents of the grocery bags. Old guides talked about a sheepherder's cottage where you could sleep on straw and have mutton for breakfast and at night a happy herder's tuneful pipe, a smile from his ample wife, and maybe more than a smile from his flaxen daughters. Vole's selection was the Pink Fluke.

We circled the cinder-block motels and plastic diners, peered through gapes in the dunes and buildings at draggers, party boats, and head boats. The piers were under metal archways, each advertising their boats like carnival sideshows. All the boats had promising names, and the captains' names were written in the jauntiest possible script. The sailing times were up there, too, a promise of diesels breaking up the thin, cold light that comes before dawn.

But there was no Pink Fluke, and there wasn't anybody about to ask. The lights were off nearly everywhere. Most people had evidently gone South and those who hadn't lay crouched behind the cinder block, waiting for the diesels. "Maybe those sheepherders of yours went too far with their grazing," said Vole. "This place is a desert fit only for growing cinder block."

"Just so long as there's fish in the water," said Holcomb.

We ran on seeking the Pink Fluke, but there was only the Blue Anchor, the Blazing Marlin, the Rose Marlin, the Prancing Billfish, the Happy Harpoon, the Deep Six, and the Ocean's Dream.

Back to the carnival arches. The captains' names looked a bit more sinister and the early sailing time downright formidable. I began to think of my days sleeping on the Delaware Bay pilot boats waiting for the dawn run out to the lighthouse off Cape May— the smell of the diesel, its sound and smell, the vibration on an empty stomach. Yeats may have written of his Connemara fisherman's cold and passionate dawn, but for me the wait seemed to promise a passion in the older Latin sense of suffering.

We headed out of town, up around the great salt pond that was the harbor, and out toward the lighthouse. On the way, of course, we passed the Pink Fluke, but it barely caused us to raise more than a mild expletive. Holcomb, to make sure there was no more of this wait-for-morning business, had moved up next to me, and Vole, showing concern for his grocery bags, had slipped into the back. "Just make sure you stop before you get to the lighthouse," he said. "Somebody told me the whole thing's going to fall over."

"If you fall off a horse," said Vole, "the trick is to get right back on." He adjusted himself in the seat, and to expand upon this hunting metaphor, rabbits continually popped across our headlights.

The beacon from the lighthouse grew so strong that we could hardly see. When Holcomb spotted a dirt road leading down the bluff, we took it, banging in the ruts like a trolley while the bayberry battled our flapping canvas.

"If you fall off a horse," stammered Holcomb, "get-right-back-up."

We made a turn that nearly sent us all off the horse, and then we were driving onto the beach. I'd already flipped the hubs to prepare the jeep for conversion to four-wheel drive, so all we had to do was grab some knobs and we were churning along with the bluff on our left and the startling white surf on our right.

There were beach buggies on the small cuspate spits of sand, points built by the current so methodically that they came up like clockwork. We slowed and tried to see if the men were catching anything, but most of them stood about with their hands in their pockets. The poles they had set in sand spikes. Holcomb figured they were using worms and sinkers, something we were not equipped for either technically or psychologically. The buggies themselves were more elaborate than anything we'd seen in Rhode Island—huge camper rigs, each its own Pink Fluke with jalousie windows, propane tanks, TV aerials and, to show what was really going on, decals of leaping bass complete with captions: "The Big Fellow Leaps" or "Unforgettable Moment." Set around the buggies were aluminum summer sizzler lawn chairs that gleamed in the weird light of Coleman lanterns hanging from aluminum poles like Japanese-beetle traps.

From time to time our headlights did pick up actual fish, or rather their skulls, and we jumped out to examine some. They seemed to be bass and must have been lunkers. So big did some of them appear that we wondered why they had been claimed by no museum, or at least by the simulated pine of an Unforgettable Den.

We came to a point with no buggy on it, and since we had no worms and there were no more suburban scenes to satirize, we began looking for a way up through the bluff. After all, we had to admit, the Pink Fluke was back there waiting for us. It was not what any of us would call an Unforgettable Moment.

It was difficult to find a way out, however. The bluff was high enough to block most of the beacon, and our own headlights bounced off the beach up ahead as if they had nothing to do with us. The only other light was the crumbling curl of the surf.

And then there were two more lights, tiny ones, close together and a little higher than we were.

"Look at him," said Holcomb.

It was a *him*, all right. Those were his eyes, and what seemed a pattern of softer lights formed a tree branch, and that dull wall under it all was his flank, and it all began moving, and there was a bobbing lantern to follow which turned into a tail as the buck moved in and out of our bounding headlights.

We turned out our lights and plowed along at about twenty miles an hour, moving finally onto the wet, hard sand so we could keep up with him. He loped about three lengths ahead of us in a crazy hobbyhorse stride that, like the movement of a porpoise, seemed more up and down than ahead. The bluff offered him no gaps, and the surf was white. Beyond it there was only blackness like the sky, for the moon had gone and with our lights out there was only that white of the surf and the white of his tail.

"That's a deer again, isn't it?" said Vole. There was barely a rattle from the grocery bags.

"Yes, it is," I said.

"Damned if it isn't nearly as good as a fish," said Holcomb.

The buck faked seaward, then, in a cut that would have left a wide receiver astonished, was across us and up into a slash in the bluff. We followed, not to torment him further, but because he had shown us the way. In the thicker sand we slowed and barely made it with all our transmissions and horsepower. Up in the bayberry the deer had shrunk into two rabbits with the same white tail, the same jumping run, and as I was thinking how the old name for rabbit was coney and that that was the name of a place on the other end of the island, the rabbits turned into cinder-block motels and metal archways, and there, as if we had now earned it, was the Pink Fluke.

It was, despite all our ferryboats and deer stalking, not yet eleven o'clock when we finished registering at the Pink Fluke. The rooms were so overheated that we opened the windows and walked out into the night where, beyond our hanging breath, we saw the lights of a building down by the docks. The door was in the corner, and we could hear voices. Mingled in the air with our breath was the smoke of a wood fire.

The stove was just inside the door, the tallest potbelly I'd ever seen, even taller than the ones you see in bridge tender's shacks along the bays and rivers of the mainland, and there was a rail around it. Along the bar were five men wearing miner's lamps. We rubbed our hands together and lined up.

The bartender seemed to be walking on a platform which presumably gave him leverage over his customers in a like manner to the placement of the wedge harpooner's stick at the end of a swordfish pulpit, the better to drive home the iron. Behind the bar, however, was the clue; in a 1940 shot of the Rochester Royals our man's present face was miraculously anticipated.

We had a couple of beers and listened to the men in miner's lamps. They were rock fishermen, not surf casters, and they were waiting, not to discover the Pink Fluke, but for the tide. Though they were after the same fish, their worries seemed as remote as those of trout fishermen in the Sierras.

We ended up talking about the deer. One of them confided to us that if we played our cards right, the bartender would steam us up some local clams. In fact there was a rumor he was doing just that, but it was all going to require a lot of cooperation and enthusiasm around midnight to make the clams a reality. Fair enough then, a story about deer for a story about clams. As for our mutual interest in bass and blues, there was no hope of exchange. They fished from rocks. We fished from sand.

While waiting for the clams, I moved up next to a man in a red mackinaw and asked him if there were still any sheepherders on the Point. He said he was from Sag Harbor way and went into a long analysis of coot and how to lure them in by painting Clorox bottles with lampblack. Vole asked him if he had known Steinbeck, and he said, "Of course. I did some of his plumbing."

The clams continued their part in the conspiracy. Steinbeck's plumber checked the door again and then signaled to the bartender who came out of the back shaking an armload of steam which he set down with a clank on the back counter. Soon each of us had a pile on the front counter, and the bartender was walking about handing out butter and fetching fresh beer. When we were all served, he collected some quarters from each of us and went to the stove with an armload of wood. Judging by the roar, it must have been pine. Soon we were sweating, and what with the heat and the beer and the shellfish, I thought of one summer at Cape May when my wife and I had eaten oysters with a bunch of geodetic surveyors and Coast Guardsmen in the Ugly Mug under a wooden fan, and everybody'd had their shoes off, and the table was piled high with shells, and the beer kept going around.

"But remember one thing," said the plumber. "Remember that when you've gone and painted your Clorox bottle decoy lampblack, that a coot's no good to eat anyhow."

The clams were, however, and we all got around with our chins in the steam and the juice and the suds. A man named Whitman, who grew up just down the road from the place, once said:

> *The boatmen and the clam-diggers arose early and stopt for me,*
> *I tuck'd my trouser-ends in my boots and went and had a good time;*
> *You should have been with us that day round the chowder-kettle.*

It came soon enough. Not the dawn, but the fierce detonations. I awoke in the dark, overheated room. Where was I? Somerset, Pennsylvania, after a hard night driving through the tunnels, the trailer trucks on all sides and only those rubber nipples between them and me and every once in a while a nipple popping up when a semi clipped it with a mud flap? No, not a tunnel, though the diesels were there all right, down in a ship, and the ship kept getting smaller and smaller as it moved out across Delaware Bay toward Cape May, and what kept popping up were rabbits in a shooting gallery full of Clorox bottles painted to look like coots. "Here you are," said Steinbeck, handing me my prize. "But remember, when you've steamed it and steamed it in the back room, a pink fluke still won't be worth eating." "I know that," I said, "I know what's in those books."

"Who turned up the heat?" said Vole. "The furnace is going to explode."

"It's not the furnace," said Holcomb, who was in a position of intellectual superiority because he was dressed. "It's the boats and they're going to be getting our fish."

"We'll be there," I said. "I know Steinbeck's plumber."

It was still dark as we bumped over the dirt road leading down to the beach. The bushes were wet enough to smell even stronger than the night before. Up ahead the road either took a sharp turn or simply went over the cliff.

"Isn't a lot of this eroded?" said Holcomb. "Isn't there a problem here about things going out to sea?"

I slowed and flicked the beams from high to low. Wasn't that what you did when driving off a cliff? There was, however, nothing out there, high or low. I stopped the jeep and, to ease the fact of there being nothing out there, I killed the lights.

"I still don't see why she had to have the heat up like that," said Vole. "I mean I spoke carefully to her about it when we came in last night." It was not especially cold in the jeep, but there was all that darkness around, and the canvas top flapped. "I mean what does a landlady get out of that kind of heat?"

"It's the cold she's afraid of," I said.

"Soon she'll be in Miami," said Holcomb.

"Miami not having quite come to Montauk," said Vole.

We sat there with the lights out. The top flopped. The engine smell began to wear off, and in the thinning smell there returned the faint bayberry and something else—of salt, and was it fish oil?

And we were neither in Miami nor quite yet Montauk, but out and down and down, slipping and skiing, and running flat out with all our gear waving and banging into some blue, chill zone beyond Montauk where the sound was of surf and in a moment a softer sound of rubber boots and still softer reel clicks and—breaking in on all the quiet—bird cries, jagged as knives.

The lighthouse was back of us, and it was using its beacon to hold itself up.

I was walking out into what the suck and kiss of my boots told me was water, ballasting myself with data about spinning rods, waders, gaffs, lures, swivels. Ahead were white streaks grating in at angles from each side to make a kind of broken chevron. Mixed in with these marks were other, smaller chevrons which I figured to be the wakes made by the boots of everyone about me as we advanced into the sea. The footing was slippery on the cobblestones, and I had all I could do to keep from having my whole body slam down on those stones. To keep on top, I imagined the stones to be humming-bird's eggs.

Around me there was talk, but a strange language, nothing about gaffs, lures, swivels, test line, but a strange language, and I wondered if perhaps it had been wrong to assume we were all fishing. Perhaps these were the shades of the old Montauk sheepherders driving their fold into the sea to escape the pursuing cinder block. There was a man at my elbow. I peered into his face. It was no one I'd ever seen before.

"Bass fishing?" I said tentatively.

"Monofilament," he mumbled and shifted his silhouette into a flapping bird.

I waded farther toward the fat chevrons. I knew what they were. I knew perfectly well what they were. The tide was out—that I could tell by the odor—and those were the waves hitting on the head of the cuspate spit. I walked right out, and with my rod cocked back, tweaked the line with my right index finger, and for maximum responsibility I cast straight overhead, counted ten, and yanked the rod tip, heard the bail click, and began cranking. Imitate, I thought, not Socrates and Jesus, as Ben Franklin advised, but, following the placard in the lure box, imitate the wounded minnow.

I put all my brain into the thoughts a wounded minnow might have as he limped in off a Montauk cuspate in November, here at the leading edge of America, and saw for the last time what the Dutch minnows who had nipped about beneath the keels of explorers Block and De Vries had first seen, that great breast of algae unpollute.

Paraphrasing Fitzgerald has gotten more than one man in over his head, and though I was at the limits of my boot tops, I decided to go a step farther. After all, there was a man ahead of me, a man I could tap with my rod, and he was breast deep, no doubt

126

equipped more adequately than I, but no holier, no more democratic. I felt the water slip in over my boots, water much colder than the Rhode Island water of a month earlier. As I grew soggy I saw the man ahead of me in the first bit of light, or pre-light, or whatever light it is when it isn't really quite there yet but is getting ready to come to us on the leading edge of America. There he is—a fellow human being at the end of what you can see, the absolute end of what you know can be, tugging at something farther out, his elbows churning in the water like an old paddle wheeler, pumping, reaching out—and he stops and plucks from in front of his chest something that in his fingers turns the darkness to silver. A fish? He lifts it over his head and digs into the water, drags up a chain that thrashes silver, a chain with two fish already on it, and with a continuous motion he adds this new fish and eases it all back into the sea. There he stands, now nearly neck deep and with three ten-pound bass swimming around his armpits, chained to him, and he raises his rod to cast again.

The beam from the lighthouse seemed to have less depth to it. That will never do, I thought, that will never hold up a tower. The air, however, was becoming thick with birds, very close—had they always been quite *that* close?

I managed to retrieve my cast three times without losing my plug, my balance, or the friendship of those around me. I was happy to retire on that, move back to knee-deep water, and there in what was first light find the dawn prefigured on the underbellies of the gulls and, in a moment, on the steel rims of the good Vole.

"I just saw . . ." I began.

"You caught—?"

"No, I—" People were jostling past us, fish jumping on their chains.

"They seem to be catching them deeper out," said Holcomb. "They have full-length waders and telephone cords on their gaffs, and after the catch they've got chains to string them on. They're properly equipped."

And then we all saw it. The sun coming up over a leaping school of bass, there at the edge of an America that was beyond all equipment.

127